Paganism:
A Study Course

A Comparison of Christianity, Norse Religions,
Buddhism, Wicca, and Reincarnation

WRITTEN AND COMPILED BY:
MARK TABATA
(EVANGELIST)

www.MarkTabata.com

Charleston, AR
COBB PUBLISHING
2023

Published in the United States of America by:
Cobb Publishing
www.CobbPublishing.com
Editor@CobbPublishing.com
479.747.8372

ISBN: 978-1-960858-12-2

Contents

Lesson One

Basic Principles

Introduction

The phrase "pagan" as we use the term today actually embraces several religious themes and ideas, almost all of them a combination of polytheism (belief in many gods and goddesses) and including various forms and blends of Hinduism, Buddhism, and witchcraft.

Yet what does the word "pagan" actually mean?

Geisler, in his article on "Neopaganism," summarizes it well:

> "Neopaganism is not a monolithic movement. It springs from the soil of paganism, "Hinduism, wicca, and, indirectly, atheism, and other systems. Modern atheism fertilized the soil out of which contemporary neopaganism grew. David Miller describes it as rising from the ashes of the "death of God" heralded by Thomas Altizer and others in the 1960s and 1970s. "The death of God gives rise to the rebirth of the gods," according to Miller. When God died in modern culture, the ancient gods rose again. Monotheism was holding back paganism. Ancient Polytheism. Of course, the main root of Neopaganism is ancient Greek and Roman polytheism....This tradition may be behind recent interest in the occult, magic, extraterrestrial life, Eastern societies and religions, communes, new forms of multiple family life, and other alternative life-style meaning systems that seem so foreign (ibid., 11).

> Hinduism. Not all modern paganism comes from Greece. The revival of "Buddhism and especially Hinduism, with its multi-millions of gods, also supports New Age religion and Neopaganism. Hinduism has infiltrated virtually every level

of Western culture, tailored to fit Western humanism by teaching that each of us is a little god. Witchcraft (Wicca) and Radical Feminism. Another stream is the religion of wicca. This movement, popularly known as witchcraft, has a strong overlap with the feminist movement. Wiccans have an abhorrence to monotheism (see THEISM). Feminist witch Margot Adler expresses this view. Adler refers to monotheism as one of the totalistic religious and political views that dominate society (Adler).

Obviously a variety of beliefs are practiced under the broad neopagan heading. There are some generally shared characteristics and beliefs that draw on polytheism, the occult, relativism, and pluralism." (Norman Geisler, Baker Encyclopedia Of Christian Apologetics, 523 (Kindle Edition); Grand Rapids, Michigan; Baker Books)

Paganism is an umbrella term that encompasses several different non-Christian philosophies and beliefs.

Does God Exist?

Pagans and Christians share common ground in acknowledging that there must be some kind of God (or gods) that transcend the material universe. Modern science confirms this in amazing ways.

For example, the famous scientist Albert Einstein (who was neither a Christian nor a pagan) describes the ways that the study of science points to a Creator.

(The following quotations are from a book written by a former atheist scientist, John M. Kinston, *Does Mathematics Point To God? Vignettes From An Ex-Atheist Scientist*, 8671-8713 (Kindle Edition)).

"The deeper one penetrates into nature's secrets, the greater becomes one's respect for God." (Einstein, as quoted in Denis Brian, Einstein: A Life, New York, John Wiley and Sons, 1996, 119).

"I want to know how God created this world. I am not interested in this or that phenomenon, in the spectrum of this

8

or that element. I want to know His thoughts, the rest are details." (Einstein, as quoted in Ronald Clark, Einstein: The Life and Times, London, Hodder and Stoughton Ltd., 1973, 33).

"My religiosity consists in a humble admiration of the infinitely superior Spirit that reveals itself in the little that we, with our weak and transitory understanding, can comprehend of reality." (Einstein 1936, as quoted in Helen Dukas, and Banesh Hoffmann, eds. Albert Einstein: The Human Side. (New Glimpses from His Archives). Princeton University Press, 1979, 66).

"Certain it is that a conviction, akin to religious feeling, of the rationality or intelligibility of the world lies behind all scientific work of a higher order. This firm belief, a belief bound up with deep feeling, in a superior Mind that reveals itself in the world of experience, represents my conception of God." (Einstein, as quoted in Ronald Clark, Einstein: The Life and Times, London, Hodder and Stoughton Ltd., 1973, 255).

"Strenuous intellectual work and the study of God's Nature are the angels that will lead me through all the troubles of this life with consolation, strength, and uncompromising rigor." (Einstein, as quoted in Alice Calaprice, ed. The Expanded Quotable Einstein. Princeton University Press, 2000, ch. 1).

"The most beautiful and most profound emotion we can experience is the sensation of the mystical. It is the sower of all true science. He to whom this emotion is a stranger, who can no longer stand rapt in awe, is as good as dead. That deeply emotional conviction of the presence of a superior Reasoning Power, which is revealed in the incomprehensible Universe, forms my idea of God." (Einstein, as quoted in Libby Anfinsen, Memorial speech for Christian Anfinsen at Memorial Garden Dedication, Weizmann Institute. November 16. The Christian Anfinsen

Papers. Profiles in Science. U.S. National Library of Medicine, 1995).

"We are in the position of a little child entering a huge library filled with books in many different languages. The child knows someone must have written those books. It does not know how. It does not understand the languages in which they are written. The child dimly suspects a mysterious order in the arrangement of the books, but doesn't know what it is. That, it seems to me, is the attitude of even the most intelligent human being toward God. We see a Universe marvelously arranged and obeying certain laws, but only dimly understand these laws. Our limited minds cannot grasp the mysterious force that moves the constellations." (Einstein, as quoted in Denis Brian, Einstein: A Life, New York, John Wiley and Sons, 1996, 186).

"Everyone who is seriously involved in the pursuit of science becomes convinced that a Spirit is manifest in the laws of the universe –a Spirit vastly superior to that of man, and one in the face of which we with our modest powers must feel humble. In this way the pursuit of science leads to a religious feeling of a special sort, which is indeed quite different from the religiosity of someone more naive." (Einstein, as quoted in Dukas and Hoffmann, Albert Einstein: The Human Side, Princeton University Press, 1979, 33).

There is indeed common ground here upon which Christians and pagans may find agreement and move forward together in our pursuit of truth.

Pagan Scriptures

Since paganism is an umbrella term which embraces numerous faiths, there are several texts which would be considered sacred to the followers of those religions. In future lessons, we will examine some of them in greater detail.

Proof

Christians believe that the Bible is the Word and that Jesus Christ is the Son of God because of various evidences and proofs which substantiate these claims.

Homer Hailey has written:

> "The function of reason per se is not to determine whether the fact was possible or impossible. Reason cannot determine whether one could begotten in the womb of a woman unimpregnated by the male sperm, or whether a dead body could be raised to life again. Rather, its function is to weigh the evidence that claims to sustain the facts. Reason must sit in judgment on the evidence and determine it valid or invalid, trustworthy or untrustworthy, strong or weak. When it has done this and has deduced a conclusion on the weight of the evidence, it has served its purpose. Will must then take over." (Homer Hailey, That You May Believe, 19; Las Vegas, Nevada; Nevada Publications).

Was Jesus Christ A Pagan?

Pagans are often taught that Jesus was Himself a pagan.

For example:

> "I then asked a question that so many wiccans avoid or revolt against, "what about Jesus?" God's reply was strong in this, "We have had children with mortals and only the purest of heart can ever bare the seed of one of us." The goddess then spoke, "We have chosen many mortals to bear what you call a demi-god. The Greeks have their myths, the Egyptians, the Norse, the Christian; all have a demi-god or more in their stories. Many of them true, they did exist. In times of great troubles, we chose a woman pure to bare a god born child. All around the world they have been born, and each have taught our truths, Arjuna, Bali, Chandra, Amphion, were each such godborns, and their spawn with mortals continued his power diluting with human blood with each generation until power was all that was left to

carry. With each godborn they each had messages similar of what we needed spoken to the people, Love, no harm, peace, forgiveness. Many spread our word and some coveted prayer to nourish them as they like you have free will. Many mysteries surround each and will always until you yourself are a being of light. Only then will you be able understand what your mortal mind cannot. Our children have had children, the holy grail is nothing but the womb of a mortal and a demigod having children that empowered a bloodline continuing grace and power. The strongest of witches are descended from what we call godborns, and what you call demigods. It explains their power, Moses split the sea for his ancestry was of us. His grandparent was an Egyptian godborn whom had power over water. Jesus had dominions over life and he too was nothing more than a godborn and he too had children, which had children, as do all godborns. There are so many generations that have passed beyond mortal memory and beyond the written word. It is why some witches are naturally stronger than others. It is divine power from us through the bloodlines. I leave you with this, Many have existed, some have been fabricated, however a true witch will know in their heart the truth. A true being with power of sight, or of mind will know and sense the truth. All paths of love lead to us and many whom lead the people back to love have a calling that is not only from us, but is in their blood as well. It is the blood of their ancestors telling them the truth and giving them the strength and power to do so." (Eric Williams (Star Soul), The Ericonian Witch's Bible: Text of the Ericonian Wiccan Tradition, 22-23 (Kindle Edition))

What are the facts?

The Proof Of Miracles

One proof that Jesus Christ is the Son of God is that He worked numerous miracles.

Mark 16:20—And they went out and preached everywhere, the Lord working with them and confirming the word through the accompanying signs. Amen.

John 3:2—This man came to Jesus by night and said to Him, "Rabbi, we know that You are a teacher come from God; for no one can do these signs that You do unless God is with him."

John 20:30-31—And truly Jesus did many other signs in the presence of His disciples, which are not written in this book; (31) but these are written that you may believe that Jesus is the Christ, the Son of God, and that believing you may have life in His name.

Acts 2:22—Men of Israel, hear these words: Jesus of Nazareth, a Man attested by God to you by miracles, wonders, and signs which God did through Him in your midst, as you yourselves also know—

Acts 2:43—Then fear came upon every soul, and many wonders and signs were done through the apostles.

Acts 5:12—And through the hands of the apostles many signs and wonders were done among the people. And they were all with one accord in Solomon's Porch.

2 Corinthians 12:12—Truly the signs of an apostle were accomplished among you with all perseverance, in signs and wonders and mighty deeds.

Hebrews 2:4—God also bearing witness both with signs and wonders, with various miracles, and gifts of the Holy Spirit, according to His own will?

The purpose of these miracles was to provide evidence and to create faith in Him and His Word.

"In at least eighteen of Jesus' miracles, faith is not present explicitly or implicitly. In some cases the faith is a result of the miracle, not a condition of it. When Jesus turned water to wine, "He thus revealed his glory, and his disciples put their faith in him" (John 2:11). Jesus 'disciples did not believe he could feed the 5000 by multiplying loaves and fishes (Luke 9:13–14; cf. Matt. 14:17). Even after they had seen Jesus feed 5000, they disbelieved he could do it again for 4000 (Matt. 15:33). In the case of the paralytic, Jesus healed him when he saw the faith of the four who carried him to Jesus, not the faith of the man himself (Mark 2:5). In seven miracles Jesus could not have required faith. This is certainly true of the three he raised from the dead. Yet Jesus raised Lazarus (John 11), the widow's son (Luke 7), and Jairus's daughter (Matthew 9). The same is true of the cursed fig tree (Matt. 21), the miracle of the tax money in the fish (Matt. 17:24–27), the two times Jesus multiplied loaves (Matt. 14:15), and his calming of the sea (Matt. 8:18–27). Neither can it be shown that faith of the disciples was required. In most cases the disciples lacked faith. In the miracle of raising Lazarus, Jesus prayed that those present might believe that God has sent him (John 11:42). Just before Jesus rebuked the waves, he said to the disciples, "Where is your faith?" (Luke 8:25). After he calmed the waters he asked, "Do you still have no faith?" (Mark 4:40). Sometimes Jesus performed miracles in spite of unbelief. The disciples lacked faith to cast the demon out of the boy (Matt. 17:14–21). Even the passage most often used to show that faith is necessary for miracles proves just the opposite. Matthew 13:58 tells us that "Jesus did not do many miracles there because of their lack of faith." However, in spite of the unbelief present, Jesus laid "his hands on a few sick people and healed them" (Mark 6:5)." (Norman L. Geisler, Baker Encyclopedia of Christian Apologetics (Baker Reference Library), 301-302 (Kindle Edition); Grand Rapids, Michigan; Baker Books)

Here is a partial list of Jesus' miracles:

- Water Turned To Wine (John 2:1)

- Many Healings (Matthew 4:23; Mark 1:32)

- Healing Of A Leper (Matthew 8:1; Mark 1:40; Luke 5:12)

14

- Healing Of A Roman Centurion's Servant (Matthew 8:5; Luke 7:1)

- Healing Of Peter's Mother-In-Law (Matthew 8:14; Mark 1:29; Luke 4:38)

- Calming Of The Storms At Sea (Matthew 8;23; Mark 4:35; Luke 8:22)

- Healing Of The Demoniacs Of Gadara (Mathew 8:28; Mark 5:1; Luke 8:26)

- Healing Of The Lame Man (Matthew 9:1; Mark 2:1; Luke 5:18)

- Healing Of A Woman With A Hemorrhage (Matthew 9:20; Mark 5:25; Luke 8:43)

- Raising Of Jairus's Daughter (Matthew 9:23; Mark 5:22; Luke 8:41)

- Healing Of Two Blind Men (Matthew 9;27)

- Healing Of A Demon Possessed Man (Matthew 9:32)

- Healing Of A Man With A Withered Hand (Matthew 12:10; Mark 3:1; Luke 6:6)

- Feeding Of 5, 000 People (Matthew 14:15; Mark 6:35; Luke 9:12; John 6:1)

- Walking On The Sea (Matthew 14:22; Mark 6:47; John 6:16)

- Healing Of The Syrophoenician's Daughter (Matthew 15:21; Mark 7:24)

- Feeding Of 4, 000 People (Matthew 15:32; Mark 8:1)

- Healing Of An Epileptic Boy (Matthew 17:14; Mark 9:14; Luke 9:37)

- Healing Of Two Blind Men At Jericho (Matthew 20:30)

- Healing Of A Man With An Unclean Spirit (Mark 1:23; Luke 4:33)

- Healing Of A Deaf Speechless Man (Mark 7:31)

- Healing Of A Blind Man At Bethesda (Mark 8:22)

- Healing Of Blind Bartimaeus (Mark 10:46; Luke 18:35)

- Miraculous Catch Of Fish (Luke 5:4)

- Raising Of A Widow's Son (Luke 7:11)

- Healing Of A Stooped Woman (Luke 13:11)

- Healing Of A Man With Dropsy (Luke 14:1)

- Healing Of Ten Lepers (Luke 17:11)

- Healing Of Malchus's Ear (Luke 22:50)

- Healing Of A Royal Official's Son (John 4:46)

- Healing Of A Lame Man At Bethesda (John 5:1)

- Healing Of A Blind Man (John 9:1)

- Raising Of Lazarus (John 11:38)

- Resurrection Of Jesus From The Dead (Matthew 28: Mark 16: Luke 24; John 21)

- Miraculous Catch Of Fish (John 21)

Other Ancient Historians Confirm the Miracles of Jesus

It is also worth noting that many non-Christian historians from the ancient world document the miracles of Christ.

"Now there was about this time Jesus, a wise man if it be lawful to call him a man, for he was a doer of wonders, a teacher of such men as receive the truth with please. He drew many after him both of the Jews and the gentiles. He was the Christ. When Pilate, at the suggestion of the principal men among us, had condemned him to the cross, those that loved him at the first did not forsake him, for he appeared to them alive again the third day, as the divine prophets had foretold these and ten thousand other wonderful things about him, and the tribe of Christians, so

16

named from him, are not extinct at this day." (Josephus, Antiquities 18:63-64)

Some object to this statement of Josephus, claiming that Christians tampered with the text. Yet the facts show the opposite!

"The rabbis and the anti-Christian Greek philosopher Celsus are clear that Jesus was a miracle worker. Of course, later non-Christian sources attributed his feats to sorcery, but that's still an acknowledgment that something extraordinary took place. Also, the first-century Jewish historian Josephus wrote that Jesus was a wise man who 'worked startling deeds." "'Startling deeds?" "Yes. What's significant is that this is the same way he describes the miracles associated with the prophet Elisha." "But isn't that passage in Josephus disputed?" I asked. "Critics charge it was added later by Christians." "The Jewish historian Geza Vermes of Oxford analyzed the writing style of Josephus and concluded that this particular miracle claim is, indeed, authentic," Keener said. 5 "Frankly, I have to agree with what scholar Raymond Brown said about Jesus, which is that even 'the oldest traditions show him as a healer." (Craig Keener in his interview with Lee Strobel, The Case For Miracles: A Journalist Investigates Evidence For The Supernatural, 85-86 (Kindle Edition); Grand Rapids, Michigan; Zondervan)

Notice some other ancient Jewish sources which document the miracles of Christ:

"On the eve of Passover Yeshu was hanged. For forty days before the execution took place, a herald went forth and cried, "He is going forth to be stoned because he has practiced sorcery and enticed Israel to apostasy. Any one who can say anything in his favour, let him come forward and plead on his behalf." But since nothing was brought forward in his favour he was hanged on the eve of the Passover!" (Babylonian Talmud)

The Talmud acknowledges Jesus' miracles and tries to ascribe them to sorcery. Of course, that Jesus' deeds were not sorcery is evident when we look at what the sorcerers of Jesus' day did. There was no comparison between the miracles of Jesus and sorcery, which is one reason we know Christ wasn't a sorcerer. Indeed, what is truly amazing is how these historical references bear witness to the miracles of Christ.

Again:

> "We learn from the Jewish sources that Jesus was the firstborn son of Mary (the rabbis). He had followers (Josephus) or gathered disciples (the rabbis); he taught them and worked miracles (Josephus, the rabbis). He was put on trial and died by formal execution (Josephus, the rabbis). Either the Jews alone carried out his trial and execution (the rabbis), or the Romans did in some cooperation with Jewish leaders (Josephus). Jesus 'followers claimed that he rose from the dead (the rabbis), and his movement continued (Josephus, the rabbis). Jesus 'brother James was a leading figure in Jerusalem after Jesus 'death (Josephus)." (Robert E. Van Voorst, Jesus Outside The New Testament: An Introduction To The Ancient Evidence, 2100-2105 (Kindle Edition); Grand Rapids, Michigan; William B. Eerdman's Publishing Company)

Then there are non-Jewish historians who bear witness to the miracles of Christ. One example is from the "Acts of Pontius Pilate," an early official document which Christians encouraged their skeptical friends to consider to prove that the miracles of Christ took place.

> "That he (Jesus, M.T.) performed these miracles you may easily satisfy yourself from the "Acts" of Pontius Pilate." (Justin Martyr, First Apology 48.3)

Regarding the Acts Of Pontius Pilate, Cooper writes:

> "The chances of a local rumour doing the rounds in Jerusalem reaching the emperor's ears back in Rome are extremely slight. To reach the emperor at all, the rumour would have to hitch a ride to Rome on the back of an official communication, and there is good evidence indeed that just such a communication was sent from Pontius Pilate to the

Emperor Tiberius about the Crucifixion and the Resurrection of our Lord. While that is not something that the critics would like to hear, it is important enough for us to consider just what this evidence is. We need firstly to bear in mind the fact that such a communication–an update on events in the province of Judaea–would be nothing extraordinary. Such communications were an expected and everyday occurrence, and woe betide the governor who neglected to send them. At the least, dereliction, treasonous thoughts or sabotage would be suspected. **Nevertheless, this report must have been something special, because it seems to have had a profound effect on Tiberius himself who received it, Tiberius putting a motion to the Senate to have this Jesus added to the gods of Rome.** Happily, the Senate declined the invitation because they'd hitherto heard nothing about this Man. We turn to Tertullian (AD 160-225) who, after describing the events leading up to the Crucifixion and Resurrection, writes: "Pilate, who in his conscience was a Christian, sent Tiberius Caesar an account of all these proceedings relating to Christ...." Earlier, but on the same general subject, he invites the recipients of his Apology to: "Consult your annals...." Now, just who was Tertullian writing to? Was it a friend or colleague?–a sympathiser of the Christians perhaps? No, by no means. He was writing to the magistrates of Carthage, to the very men who were then persecuting the Christians. **To invite them to consult the state archives to test the truth of what he was saying was a brave move-and a foolish one if the annals had not existed, or had told a story contrary to his own.** But this same record is also mentioned by a slightly earlier apologist of the Christian faith, Justin Martyr (AD 100-165): "... and for the truth of this you may satisfy yourselves from the acts of Pontius Pilate...." Again the invitation to consult the state archives. Who was Justin writing to?-none other than the emperor of Rome at that time, Antoninus Pius, his sons, and the Senate of Rome. **That again is quite a readership, and Justin would have been the most foolish man on earth to invite a hostile** emperor to consult the archives on Pontius Pilate if those records had not been there to consult. **Moreover, those archives must have held papers on the Crucifixion of Jesus and His subsequent Resurrection, including a report on the rumour that Matthew records about the disciples being thought to have stolen His body.** It's a wonder that the critics forget to mention these things. But there's more. Eusebius, expanding on the subject, tells us: "Tiberius, therefore, under whom the name of Christ was spread throughout the world, when this doctrine was announced to him from Palestine where it first began, communicated with the senate, being obviously pleased with the doctrine; but the senate, as they had not proposed the measure, rejected it. But he continued in his opinion, threatening death to the accusers of the Christians; a divine providence infusing this into his mind, that the gospel, having freer scope in its commencement, might spread everywhere over the world." And it did spread everywhere too under Tiberius, as we know from the evidence concerning the Lady Pomponia and the arrival of the Gospel in Britain whilst Tiberius still reigned. But regarding the report sent by Pilate to Tiberius, it is important to consider this. Our secret and intelligence services get to know that things are about to happen by listening to 'chatter' on the internet and mobile phone networks, and what we have just examined is precisely the same kind of chatter that they listen to. **In other words, what we have just read about the report from Pilate in Justin, Tertullian and Eusebius, would not be there for us to read unless that report had at one time existed, and had been available in the state archives for others to consult some two hundred years or more afterwards. It is as simple and as straightforward as that. The critics can howl that it isn't true till they're blue in the face if they wish, but eggs is eggs, and facts are facts!"** (Bill Cooper, The Authenticity Of The New Testament: Part One-The Gospels, 1274-1316 (Kindle Edition, emphasis added, M.T.).

Jesus Christ Was Not A Pagan Sorcerer

It is also helpful to observe just here that the pagans of Jesus' day were able to recognize very clearly the difference between the sorcery of pagan religions and the miracles done in the name of Christ Jesus.

> *Acts 8:4-19—Therefore those who were scattered went everywhere preaching the word. (5) Then Philip went down to the city of Samaria and preached Christ to them. (6) And the multitudes with one accord heeded the things spoken by Philip, hearing and seeing the miracles which he did. (7) For unclean spirits, crying with a loud voice, came out of many who were possessed; and many who were paralyzed and lame were healed. (8) And there was great joy in that city. (9) But there was a certain man called Simon, who previously practiced sorcery in the city and astonished the people of Samaria, claiming that he was someone great, (10) to whom they all gave heed, from the least to the greatest, saying, "This man is the great power of God." (11) And they heeded him because he had astonished them with his sorceries for a long time. (12) But when they believed Philip as he preached the things concerning the kingdom of God and the name of Jesus Christ, both men and women were baptized. (13) Then Simon himself also believed; and when he was baptized he continued with Philip, and was amazed, seeing the miracles and signs which were done. (14) Now when the apostles who were at Jerusalem heard that Samaria had received the word of God, they sent Peter and John to them, (15) who, when they had come down, prayed for them that they might receive the Holy Spirit. (16) For as yet He had fallen upon none of them. They had only been baptized in the name of the Lord Jesus. (17) Then they laid hands on them, and they received the Holy Spirit. (18) And when Simon saw that through the laying on of the apostles' hands the Holy Spirit was given, he offered them money, (19) saying, "Give me this power also, that anyone on whom I lay hands may receive the Holy Spirit."*

McGarvey comments on this passage:

"Suffice it to say, that this single incident should put to silence forever that species of skepticism which resolves all the miracles of Christ and the apostles into occult art and optical illusions; for here are these arts, in their most delusive form, brought into direct conflict with apostolic miracles; and so palpable is the distinction, that it is at once discovered and acknowledged by the whole multitude." (J.W. McGarvey, A Commentary on Acts of the Apostles, With a Revised Version of the Text, 7th Edition (With Active Table of Contents), 2383-2387 (Kindle Edition))

It is worthy of note that while many claim Jesus was a pagan sorcerer, no other sorcerer of antiquity (or of modern times) can perform the miracles that He did!

Thiede well points out:

"In AD 178, one of the fiercest critics of nascent Christianity, a certain Celsus (Kelsos in Greek), a man who disputed the validity of the Christian message with every philosophical and pseudo-rational argument he could muster, never for a moment doubted the historicity of Jesus 'miracles. They had all happened–but, Celsus alleged, Jesus had learned the art of miraculous healings and other such deeds when he stayed in Egypt as a young boy and was taught by Egyptian magicians. If this was so, it remains to be asked why Egyptian magicians themselves never performed such miracles." (Peter Thiede, Jesus, Man or Myth? 63 (Kindle Edition); Oxford, England; Lion Books)

The miracles of Christ validate His claims and demonstrate that He is not a pagan sorcerer.

Proof Of The Bible

In the same way, Christians point to numerous evidences from the Bible itself which demonstrate that it is the Word of God (i.e., the astonishing ability of the Prophets of the Bible to describe in shocking clarity future events which were beyond their ability to see and which came to pass, the supernatural unity of the Bible, the amazing foreknowledge of scientific truths which we in our day and age are just now beginning to grasp, etc.).

We will examine the scriptures of the various pagan religious mentioned above in greater detail in future lessons; yet suffice it to say here, the Bible is in a class by itself regarding verifiable evidences of Divine inspiration.

It is because we can recognize the Divine inspiration of the Bible from the aforementioned evidences that we can trust it to be a reliable guide (2 Timothy 3:16-17).

With that in mind, what does the Bible teach about the existence of the various gods and goddesses of paganism?

Does The Bible Teach That There Are Many Gods?

It is a shock to many people (including many Christians) to learn that the Bible actually discusses the existence and reality of other gods in addition to the God of the Bible.

For example, when God was describing His punishment of the Egyptians, He declares:

> *Exodus 12:12—For I will pass through the land of Egypt on that night, and will strike all the firstborn in the land of Egypt, both man and beast; and against all the gods of Egypt I will execute judgment: I am the LORD."*

Indeed, the Bible teaches in numerous places that there are multiple gods/goddesses.

Please consider:

> *Exodus 15:11—Who is like You, O LORD, among the gods? Who is like You, glorious in holiness, Fearful in praises, doing wonders?*

> *Exodus 18:11—Now I know that the LORD is greater than all the gods; for in the very thing in which they behaved proudly, He was above them."*

> *Exodus 20:3- "You shall have no other gods before Me.*

Numbers 33:4—For the Egyptians were burying all their firstborn, whom the LORD had killed among them. Also on their gods the LORD had executed judgments.

Deuteronomy 10:17—For the LORD your God is God of gods and Lord of lords, the great God, mighty and awesome, who shows no partiality nor takes a bribe.

Psalm 82:1—God stands in the congregation of the mighty; He judges among the gods.

Psalm 86:8—Among the gods there is none like You, O Lord; Nor are there any works like Your works.

Psalm 95:3—For the LORD is the great God, And the great King above all gods.

Psalm 96:4—For the LORD is great and greatly to be praised; He is to be feared above all gods.

Psalm 135:5—For I know that the LORD is great, And our Lord is above all gods.

Many other Scriptures from both Old and New Testaments elaborate on this fact.

Doesn't The Bible Teach That There Is Only One God?

Some may object, "No, the Bible teaches there is only one God."

Perhaps they are thinking of passages like this:

Isaiah 44:6-"Thus says the LORD, the King of Israel, And his Redeemer, the LORD of hosts: 'I am the First and I am the Last; Besides Me there is no God."

Many passages of Scripture teach that there are other gods besides Jehovah (i.e., the God of the Bible). Yet some passages teach that there are no other gods besides the God of the Bible.

Is there a contradiction here?

Not at all.

24

Very simply, different words can carry different meanings and definitions. We are able to tell what a word means by several clues, including the context in which it is found.

We recognize this principle and apply it to our lives daily.

When the Bible talks about there being no god "besides" the God of the Bible, it means that there is only one TRUE God, not that other "gods" do not exist. Michael Heiser explains this very well:

> "Another misguided strategy is to argue that statements in the Old Testament that have God saying "there is none besides me" mean that no other elohim exist. This isn't the case. These phrases do not contradict Psalm 82 or others that, for example, say Yahweh is above all elohim or is the "God of gods [elohim]." I've written a lot on this subject— it was a focus of my doctoral dissertation. These "denial statements," as they are called by scholars, do not assert that there are no other elohim. In fact, some of them are found in chapters where the reality of other elohim is affirmed. We've already seen that Deuteronomy 32:17 refers to elohim that Paul believed existed. Deuteronomy 32:8–9 also refers to the sons of God. Deuteronomy 4:19–20 is a parallel to that passage, and yet Deuteronomy 4:35 says there is no god besides Yahweh. Is Scripture filled with contradictions? No. These "denial statements" do not deny that other elohim exist. Rather, they deny that any elohim compares to Yahweh. They are statements of incomparability. This point is easily illustrated by noticing where else the same denial language shows up in the Bible. Isaiah 47:8 and Zephaniah 2:15 have, respectively, Babylon and Nineveh saying "there is none besides me." Are we to believe that the point of the phrase is to declare that no other cities exist except Babylon or Nineveh? That would be absurd. The point of the statement is that Babylon and Nineveh considered themselves incomparable, as though no other city could measure up to them. This is precisely the point when these same phrases are used of other gods—they cannot measure up to Yahweh. The Bible does not contradict itself on this

point. Those who want to argue that the other elohim do not exist are at odds with the supernatural worldview of the biblical writers." (Michael S. Heiser, Unseen Realm: Recovering The Supernatural Worldview Of The Bible, 571-595 (Kindle Edition); Bellingham, WA; Lexham Press)

One True God

The Bible is clear that there are indeed many gods and goddesses:

1 Corinthians 8:5-6-"It's really not important if there are things called gods in heaven or on earth—and there are many of these "gods" and "lords" out there. (6) For us there is only one God, and he is our Father. All things came from him, and we live for him. And there is only one Lord, Jesus Christ. All things were made through him, and we also have life through him."

However, the Bible is also clear that there is only one TRUE God.

There is only one eternal God Who has always existed! Not only is this the teaching of Scripture, but it is the only logical conclusion drawn from the evidence of nature.

One author has written:

"We know from the cosmological and divine design (teleological) evidences of the universe that God must be infinite because He created all space, all time and all matter from nothing. Infinite simply means that He is self- existent, non- spatial, immaterial, timeless, personal, unimaginably powerful and supremely intelligent etc. In other words, there is nothing lacking in Him. The fact that God is infinite impliedly rules out all pantheistic religions such as the New Age Movement, Hinduism and some forms of Buddhism that equate God to the universe as we have seen that universe is not infinite as it had a beginning and was designed by another cause. This fact also disproves polytheistic religions (the belief that there are many gods) such as Mormonism, as there logically cannot be more than one omnipresent infinite being. Let me explain more simply: If there was more than one God (e.g. God "A" and God "B"), then to distinguish one from the other they must differ in some way. If God "A" is infinite then God "B" must be less than infinite (i.e. infinite minus something), as the definition of infinite means that God "A" lacks nothing. Therefore, if God "B" is less than infinite he is not God! Therefore, we can only logically conclude that there can only be one Infinite Being or God who is transcendent or outside all time, all space and all matter." (Paul Ferguson, God And The Atheist: A Lawyer Assesses The Evidence For The Existence Of God, 1133-1144 (Kindle Edition); Greenville,, South Carolina; Ambassador International)

In order for there to be a measurable difference between the "gods," then one or more would need to be imperfect. Yet imperfection demands something greater than itself by which the imperfection is measured. Therefore, the "imperfect" cannot truly be God.

So there is only one true God.

Yet if there is only one TRUE god, then who (or WHAT) are the other gods and goddesses mentioned in the Bible?

According to the Bible, God created another group of intelligent creatures besides humanity which are known as angels.

Psalm 104:4—Who makes His angels spirits, His ministers a flame of fire.

Hebrews 1:14—Are they not all ministering spirits sent forth to minister for those who will inherit salvation?

The angels of God are often called "sons of God" throughout the Bible (Genesis 6:1-4; Job 1:6; 2:1; 38:4-7). Indeed, we are told that many of these angels at one time rebelled against God, being led by another fallen angel named Satan.

Revelation 12:3-12—And another sign appeared in heaven: behold, a great, fiery red dragon having seven heads and ten horns, and seven diadems on his heads. 4 His tail drew a third of the stars of heaven and threw them to the earth. And the dragon stood before the woman who was ready to give birth, to devour her Child as soon as it was born. (5) She bore a male Child who was to rule all nations with a rod of iron. And her Child was caught up to God and His throne. (6) Then the woman fled into the wilderness, where she has a place prepared by God, that they should feed her there one thousand two hundred and sixty days. (7) And war broke out in heaven: Michael and his angels fought with the dragon; and the dragon and his angels fought, (8) but they did not prevail, nor was a place found for them in heaven any longer. (9) So the great dragon was cast out, that serpent of old, called the Devil and Satan, who deceives the whole world; he was cast to the earth, and his angels were cast out with him. (10) Then I heard a loud voice saying in heaven, "Now salvation, and strength, and the kingdom of our God, and the power of His Christ have come, for the accuser of our brethren, who accused them before our God day and night, has been cast down. (11) And they overcame him by the blood of the Lamb and by the word of their testimony, and they did not love their lives to the death. (12) Therefore rejoice, O heavens, and you who dwell in them! Woe to the inhabitants of the earth and the sea! For the devil has come down to you, having great wrath, because he knows that he has a short time."

Now, according to the Psalms, God addresses the pagan gods and goddesses....and identifies them as these fallen angels!

Psalm 82:1, 6—God stands in the congregation of the mighty; He judges among the gods....I said, "You are gods, And all of you are children of the Most High.

The gods and goddesses of the pagan religions are the fallen angels who rebelled against the one true God.

The grace of the Lord Jesus Christ, and the love of God, and the communion of the Holy Spirit, be with you all. Amen.

Questions

1. According to Psalm 82, who are the gods and goddesses of the pagan religions?

   _____

2. What are some ways that we know there is only one true God?

   _____

   _____

   _____

3. What was the purpose of miracles?

   _____

   _____

4. List some of the ancient non-biblical historians and historical documents which document the miracles of Jesus Christ.

   _____

   _____

   _____

5. What does Revelation 12:3-12 teach us about Satan?

   _____

   _____

   _____

6. What does the word "pagan" have reference to?

   _____

   _____

7. "We are in the position of a little child entering a huge _____ filled with books in many different languages. The child knows _____ must have written those books. It does not know how. It does not understand the _____ in which they are written. The child dimly suspects a mysterious order in the arrangement of the books, but doesn't know what it is. That, it seems to me, is the attitude of even the most

_____ human being toward _____. We see a
Universe marvelously _____ and _____
certain _____, but only dimly understand these laws.
Our limited minds cannot grasp the _____
_____ that moves the _____."
(Einstein, as quoted in Denis Brian, Einstein: A Life, New
York, John Wiley and Sons, 1996, 186).

Lesson Two

Norse Paganism (One)

The religion known as Asatro (also known as Asatru) is the worship and veneration of the Norse gods. These were the gods primarily worshipped by the Scandinavian peoples (known generally as the Vikings).

"WHO AND WHAT WERE THE VIKINGS? Those at the receiving end of attacks from the north used various names for those responsible. In Anglo-Saxon written sources, the terms "Danes", "Northmen", "pagans" or "heathens" were most often used. What is intriguing is that the term "Danes" did not carry much geographical accuracy. Consequently, when we read "Danes" in the accounts of a particular raid we cannot be certain that those responsible actually came from Denmark. For example, in one report of a raid on Portland, Dorset, in 789, the same entry says they were Danes–yet they came from Norway. The Franks (in what is now France and western Germany) called them the Nordmanni (Northmen) and so an area ceded to them in the tenth century would become Normandy (land of the Northmen). Slavs knew them from their ruddy complexions as the Rus (red) and a related word, Rhos, was used by the Byzantines, who employed them as mercenaries and met Scandinavians who had travelled down the rivers leading into the Black Sea and on into the eastern Mediterranean and the Byzantine Empire. This latter word (in the form Rus) would eventually give rise to the name of Russia: what started as a mixed Viking/ Slav state centred on Kiev was at the core of the early Russian nation. The Byzantines also called them Varangians (those who swear loyalty) and the mercenaries of the Varangian Guard served the Byzantine emperor in Constantinople. Then in Ireland they were the Lochlannach (Northmen), a designation similar to the one used by the Franks. The Irish went on to differentiate between the Norwegians as Finn-gaill (white foreigners) and the Danes as Dubh-gaill (black foreigners), which will be explained in Chapter 5. Far from Scandinavia, Islamic writers called them al-madjus (heathens) in a religiously derived label similar to that used by Anglo-Saxons. What is surprising to the modern reader is the fact that we hardly ever hear them called Vikings outside of Scandinavia. So where does the familiar term Viking come from? There is no definite answer as the term may have had a number of possible origins. In Old Icelandic (a variant of the Old Norse language) the word vík (bay, creek) may have been used to describe seamen hiding in, or sailing from, these coastal inlets, so a geographical term may have become a group name. In addition, an area of southern Norway was called Vik, so this may have become attached to those sailing from this area. Then again, the Old Icelandic verb víkja (moving, turning aside) may have come to describe seafarers who were always "on the move". Old Norse Scandinavian written sources (which appear very late in Scandinavia) call a raider a víkingr, and a raiding expedition of such men a víking. This reminds us that "the word 'Viking 'is something you did rather than what you were" 1". (Martyn Whittock & Hannah Whittock, The Vikings: From Odin to Christ, 8-9 (Kindle Edition); Oxford, England; Lion Hudson Limited)

There were many Viking gods. The most famous was Odin (whose name carries with it the meaning of "the possessed one" or something similar), and his wife Frigg. Odin's most well-known son was Thor.

In this study, we will focus on these three beings.

The Scriptures Of The Norse Religion

The two primary sources of Norse scripture are the Poetic Eddas and the Prose Eddas. The Poetic Eddas were preserved by Sæmund

Sigfusson, and the Prose Eddas were preserved by his adopted grandson, Snorri Sturluson.

"Scholars continue to examine and analyze the historical roots of ancient and medieval deities, but it's also important to attempt to understand exactly how these deities were viewed and worshiped by their followers. Regardless of the true explanation for the origins of certain gods, the people who followed them obviously had their own explanations regarding the origins of these deities as well. In the case of the Norse gods, there are several surviving myths and legends, particularly the two exceptional collections of Norse mythology called the Eddas. There are also other sources, including Icelandic sagas and other smaller documents. The "Eddas" are medieval texts that explain the origins, adventures and ultimate fates of the gods, as well as tales about the origins of the world and similar subjects. The first of the Eddas is called the "Elder" or "Poetic" Edda, because it is older and written in poetic form, while the other is the "Younger" or "Prose" Edda. While both are immensely important for understanding Odin, there are some significant differences between them. The Poetic Edda is composed of a series of poems which probably existed for some time among the Norse before they were written down around the late 11th century. While there is no way to confirm their exact author, tradition states that they were collected by Sæmund Sigfusson, who was a descendant of the famous King Harald Hildetonn. If Sæmund did pen the book, he would have made a perfect author; his high status family gave him the opportunity for an education in the old tales and also provided him with the wealth to travel, which he did throughout Europe. And fortunately for posterity, Sæmund was born about 50 years before the institution of Christianity as the official religion of Iceland, which meant he could have learned the tales in a public setting without fear of persecution. It is known that in addition to the possible authorship of the Edda, Sæmund also wrote extensively on the history and poetry of his people and was reputed (in folklore even to this day) to be a sorcerer skilled in protective magics. Though it is unknown whether Sæmund was a believer, his status as a "sorcerer" and his interest in these tales indicate that he very well may have been and might have imagined the Edda as a document comparable to and in competition with the Christian Bible. True to its name, the Poetic Edda is composed of a series of thematic poems which are divided into two sections, the Mythological (which deals with the stories of the creation of the world and the gods) and the Heroic (which deals with the tales of the deeds of humans). Naturally, Odin features prominently in many of these tales, such as the Völuspá, an account of the creation and eventual fate of the world. In Völuspá, the narrator-a seeress-is explicitly telling her tale to Odin, so the tale not only revolves around Odin and his family but makes the god the official audience of the story. He also looms large in the Hávamál, the Lokasenna, the Lokasenna and the Hárbarðsljóð, all poems that are explored in greater detail below. The Prose Edda is at least a century younger than the Poetic Edda and has been authoritatively attributed to Snorri Sturluson, another prominent Icelander who lived from 1178-1241 and was twice the lawspeaker (a type of supreme magistrate) of the Medieval Commonwealth of Iceland. There is a direct connection between Snorri's work and that of Saemund. As a young man, Snorri was fostered to the grandson of Saemund, a learned scholar who lived in the same region as Saemund and undoubtedly had access to his ancestor's writings. Naturally, Snorri learned history from his foster father and cites the poems of the Poetic Edda numerous times in his work. He attempted to convert the disparate Norse songs and poems into a cohesive prose work, as well as adding an introduction and conclusion. The Prose Edda differs in a number of important ways from the Poetic Edda, and while it is important to the study of Norse myths, it is sometimes considered to be the less valuable source. The work takes the form of prose stories, which is probably a change in genre from the original poems connected to the oral tradition, but Snorri references the Elder Edda a number of times and obviously used it as a source (though not his only one). Snorri clearly had access to traditional tales and writings, but he was undeniably a Christian and attempts in his book to explain away Norse mythology using the Euhemerist logic. Since Iceland was now Christian, Snorri likely did not have the same public access to the tales that Sæmund would have had generations earlier; in the mid-13th century, the Norse myths were considered a subject of historical research, not a living tradition. If the Prose Edda were simply a retelling of tales, it would not warrant attention, but there are tales about Odin and the other gods in this book which only survive in it, thus making it an invaluable source. The Prose Edda is divided into three main parts (besides a commentary prologue): the Gylfaginning (The "Tricking of Gylfi"), the Skáldskaparmál (" The Language of Poetry") and the Háttatal (a "List of Verse Forms"). The first details the stories of the Norse gods-including the creation of the world and the events of Ragnarok-within the framework of a human (King Gylfi) being tricked by a mysterious trio of beings and forced to answer their questions. The Skáldskaparmál and Háttatal are structured more as guides to poetic forms than collections of tales and do not relate directly to the stories of the gods. Both of the Eddas relate the creation of the world, a series of events in which Odin was closely connected. By comparing and combining the two, readers can reach a clear understanding of these early days. The Gylfaginning questions open with Odin, his names and his glory, and then turns to his origins: "Then said Gangleri: 'What did he before heaven and earth were made? 'And Hárr answered: 'He was then with the Rime-Giants. ' Gangleri said: 'What was the beginning, or how began it, or what was before it? 'Hárr answered: 'As is told in Völuspá: Erst was the age | when nothing was: Nor sand nor sea, | nor chilling stream-waves; Earth was not found, | nor Ether-Heaven,—A Yawning Gap, | but grass was none. 'Then said Jafnhárr: 'It was many ages before the earth was shaped that the Mist-World was made...'" The Gylfaginning III-IV, from the Prose Edda The tales describe the early world as one of fire, ice and mist that was largely populated by the rime giants, beings who would be Odin's bitter enemies until the end of his life. These beings descended from a particularly mighty giant named Ymir, who was created by the coalescence of the icy mists and the primordial fire. Odin and his two brothers, on the other hand, are descendants of the god Búri, who was born out of the ice." (Jesse Harasta & Charles River Editors, Odin and Thor: The Origins, History and Religious Evolution of the Norse Gods, 305-383 (Kindle Edition); Charles River Editors)

Most of our information of the Norse religion comes from these two books.

The Nine Realms

According to the Eddas, the universe is divided up into The Nine Realms.

One author (Matt Clayton, Norse Mythology: Captivating Stories Of The Gods, Sagas And Heroes, 1675-1686 (Kindle Edition)) provides much of the material for the following chart:

Chart Of The Nine Realms

Asgard—(World Of The Aesir (Norse) Gods)
Midgard—(The Home Of Mankind/Middle Earth)
Vanaheim—Terriroty Of The Vanir Gods. Possible That Frigg (Odin's Wife) Was From This Realm
Jotunheim—The World Of The Giants. Claimed That Loki (Thor's Prankster Brother) Was Adopted From The Descendants Of This Realm
Niflheim—A Primitive World Of Ice
Muspelheim—Horrible World Of Fire

Alfheim—The Realm Of The Elves
Svartalfheim—The Land Of The Dwarves
Hel—The Realm Of The Dead and Overseen By A Goddess

Let's Start With Odin

The first god we will examine in the Norse pantheon is the being known as Odin.

Divine Or Human?

In the Prose Edda, we find this interesting note:

"The lineage of Sif I cannot tell; she was fairest of all women, {p. 7} and her hair was like gold. Their son was Lóridi, who resembled his father; his son was Einridi, his son Vingethor, his son Vingener, his son Móda, his son Magi, his son Seskef, his son Bedvig, his son Athra (whom we call Annarr), his son Ítermann, his son Heremód, his son Skjaldun (whom we call Skjöld), his son Bjáf (whom we call Bjárr), his son Ját, his son Gudólfr, his son Finn, his son Fríallaf (whom we call Fridleifr); his son was he who is named Vóden, whom we call Odin: he was a man far-famed for wisdom and every accomplishment. His wife was Frígídá, whom we call Frigg....

And wherever they went over the lands of the earth, many glorious things were spoken of them, so that they were held more like gods than men." (Snorri Sturlson, Prose Edda (Translated by Arthur Gilchrist Brodeur), 11 (Kindle Edition)

As noted above, Snori Sturlson was a researcher living in the tenth-eleventh centuries A.D. who wrote down the legends of the Norse pantheon. By his time, manny of the Scandinavians had "converted" to Catholicism. As such, Sturlson's writings reflect the belief long held by many in his day that the Norse gods were actually deified human beings.

Scholar Jesse Harasta notes the fact that this viewpoint has much evidence to document its' claims regarding the origin of the pagan gods and goddesses, although he himself is skeptical about this possible explanation for the origin of the Norse gods:

"The Euhemerists are named after an early Christian figure named Euhermerus, who theorized that the Greek pantheon was in fact the deification of long-dead war leaders. Euhermerus argued that the Greek deities were in fact ancient human kings and heroes transformed into gods through the process of centuries of retelling and exaggeration. The Euhemerist position was a common one taken by early Christian polemicists fighting against Greek and Roman paganism, and it was well-known to any Medieval European Christian scholar, especially those who studied (and argued against) the Norse Heathen pantheon. The early Christian Norse scholars began to use Euhemerism as an argument against the Heathens, and the two most important writers in this area were Saxo Grammaticus and Snorri Sturluson, the author of the Prose Edda. Snorri proposed his Euhemerist theory in the Prose Edda when he explained his belief that Odin and Thor and the other gods were once mortal humans, and that the sites of their tombs became places of worship over the centuries. Snorri believed that the Aesir were a group of people who lived in a city called Asgard in Western Asia and that their king-Odin-led them westward into the Germanic lands to found a new kingdom. 18th century manuscript of Snorri's Prose Edda Saxo went even further, giving a more elaborate story. He believed that Odin was the king of Uppsala, and that he had encouraged his people to worship him as a god, to the point of having a golden idol made of himself for the temple. His wife, Frigg, along with her lover (a servant), stole the gold and forced Odin into exile. A sorcerer took his place and attempted to create his own cult, but eventually Odin returned and cast him out. The site of his tomb in Uppsala became a sacred place, which it continued to be until the end of the Heathen era. Uppsala was the ceremonial center of the Heathen Swedish kingdoms, with splendid temples in Saxo's days as well as the tombs of the royal families, all of which added to his argument. The Euhemerist authors of the early Christian and Medieval period had reason to believe that ancient kings would set themselves up as gods, and that they might be worshiped by their descendants. After all, they could simply point to the Roman Emperors. The Imperial Cult was the state religion of Rome between the founding of the Empire and its conversion to Christianity, and emperors were said to have divine guidance and, after their death, could be elevated to godhood by a vote in the Roman Senate. Some Romans who were elevated in this way included Julius Caesar and his heir Augustus. It served as a crucial element in holding the Roman Empire together, and it was bitterly opposed by the Early Christians. They could point to the human origins of Caesar and Augustus, and no doubt it was easy to theorize there was a similar explanation for the deification of gods like Zeus and Odin. In a similar vein, it's possible that actual historical figures were integrated into mythology. For example, Achilles may not have actually fought at Troy, but historians are virtually certain there was a Trojan War, and it would make sense for the figures in Homer's Iliad to be based off actual stories of the war that at least had some basis in fact. There is, however, little direct evidence that suggests pantheons of gods were based on actual historical figures. Thus, this theory about actual historical figures probably does not explain the origins of the Norse gods, at least not comprehensively." (Jesse Harasta & Charles River Editors, Odin and Thor: The Origins, History and Religious Evolution of the Norse Gods, 198-232 (Kindle Edition); Charles River Editors)

There is a great deal of historical evidence which undergirds the idea that the Norse gods were actually deified human beings. Indeed, much of the material from the church fathers regarding these matters predates the research of Euhermerus by centuries!

In examining the various histories of the world (and how they point undeniably to the account of Noah and the Table of Nations in the Bible), Ken Johnson has documented:

"Six ancient manuscripts still preserve the linage of the Scandinavian people of Denmark, Sweden, Norway, Iceland, and the Anglo-Saxons....

"These six histories show a combined list of twenty generations from Noah to Odin. Scholars have long noted that the Scandinavians refer to Japheth, Noah's son, as Sceaf....

"The twentieth generation is Oden or Woden. Oden was the principle ancestor worshiped as a god by the pagan Scandinavians.". (Ken Johnson, Th.D., Ancient Post-Flood History: Historical Documents That Point To Biblical Creation, 2378-2435 (Kindle Edition))

Later, in explaining the research of the church fathers into these matters, Johnson noted:

"In order to spread the gospel, the early church fathers (Lactantius and several others) started researching history books that were already very ancient in t heir time. These included the history books of Herodotus, Strabo, Sanchoniathon, Ennius and others. The church fathers discovered the "gods" were simply deified men. The fathers identified where the "gods" actually ruled, died, and where they were buried....

"What we should take from this history is that, as Christians, we need to find the truth behind the myths and legends of false religions and cults. The church fathers dug up all this history from books already ancient in their time. They wanted to show from the sacred texts of the Greeks and Romans that their gods are simply deified men. Why worship what you know are not gods but just dead men? This information helped Christians take over the pagan Roman Empire. We can use the same method today. If we expose the real history behind the false religions and cults from their own "sacred" texts, we will have a stronger chance to convert unbelievers." (Ken Johnson, Th.D., Ancient Post-Flood History: Historical Documents That Point To Biblical Creation, 2846-2995 (Kindle Edition)

Johnson is correct in the meticulous research that the church fathers did in their examination of the origins of the "gods" of the pagans....and also of noting their deaths (even where they were buried)!

Here are a few examples of this evidence. (The following quotations are taken from David Bercot, A Dictionary Of Early Christian Belief: A Reference Guide To More Than 700 Topics Discussed By The Early Church Fathers (Kindle Edition); Peabody, Massachusetts; Hendrickson Publishers Marketing, LLC)

"I will further write and show, as far as my ability goes, how and for what causes images were made to kings and tyrants, and how they came to be regarded as gods. The people of Argos made images to Hercules, because he belonged to their city. Furthermore, he was strong, and by his valor, he slew noxious beasts. Besides that, they were afraid of him. For he was subject to no control, and he carried off the wives of many. His lust was great, like that of Zuradi the Persian, his friend. Again, the people of Acte worshipped Dionysius, a king, because he had recently planted the vine in their country. The Egyptians worshipped Joseph the Hebrew, who was called Serapis, because he supplied them with corn during the years of famine. (Melito (c. 170, E), 8.752)

"I maintain, then, that it was Orpheus, Homer, and Hesiod who gave both genealogies and names to those whom they call gods. Such, too, is the testimony of Herodotus. "My opinion," he says, "is that Hesiod and Homer preceded me by four hundred years, and no more. And it was they who framed a theogony for the Greeks, and gave the gods their names. It was they who assigned them their various honors and functions, and described their forms." (Athenagoras (c. 175, E), 2.136.)

"The gods, as they affirm, were not from the beginning. Rather, every one of them has come into existence just like ourselves." (Athenagoras (c. 175, E), 2.137.)

"Not one of your gods is earlier than Saturn. From him, you trace all your deities, even those of higher rank and greater fame.... Yet, none of the writers about sacred antiquities have ventured to say that Saturn was anything but a man." (Tertullian (c. 197, W), 3.26)

"As you cannot deny that these deities of yours once were men, you have taken it on yourselves to assert that they were made gods after their deaths." (Tertullian (c. 197, W), 3.27)

"As we have already shown, every god depended on the decision of the senate for his deity." (Tertullian (c. 197, W), 3.29)

"That those are no gods whom the common people worship, is known from this: They were formerly kings. On account of their royal memory, they subsequently began to be adored by their people even in death. Later, temples were founded to them. Next, images were sculptured to retain the faces of the deceased by such likenesses. Later, men sacrificed victims and celebrated festal days to give them honor. Finally, those rites became sacred to posterity— although at first they had been adopted as a consolation." (Cyprian (c. 250, W), 5.465.)

"Since it is evident from these things that they were men, it is not difficult to see how they began to be called gods. For apparently there were no kings before Saturn or Uranus. Rather, men existed in small numbers, and they lived a rural life without any ruler. Undoubtedly, then, in those days, men began to exalt the king himself and his whole family with the highest praises and with new honors—so that they even called them gods." (Lactantius (c. 304–313, W), 7.26.)

"Different people privately honored the founders of their nation or city with the highest veneration—whether they were men distinguished for bravery, or women admirable for chastity. So the Egyptians honored Isis; the Moors,

Juba;... the Romans, Quirinus. In the same exact manner, Athens worshipped Minerva; Samos, Juno; Paphos, Venus;... and Delos, Apollo. And thus various sacred rites were undertaken among different peoples and countries. For men desire to show gratitude to their rulers.... Moreover, the piety of their successors contributed largely to this error. For, in order that they might appear to be born from a divine origin, men paid divine honors to their parents." (Lactantius (c. 304–313, W), 7.27.)

"[Others, however,] not only admit that gods have been made from men, but even boast of it as a subject of praise. [Such humans have been deified] either because of their valor (as in the case of Hercules), or because of their gifts (as Ceres and Liber), or because of the arts that they discovered (as Aesculapius or Minerva). But how foolish these things are! How unworthy of being the causes of why men should contaminate themselves with inexpiable guilt, and become enemies of God. For it is in contempt of Him that they make offerings to the dead." (Lactantius (c. 304–313, W), 7.30)

"We can show that all those whom you represent to us as gods, and whom you call gods, were actually men. We can do this by quoting either Euhererus of Acragas... or Nicanor the Cyprian." (Arnobius (c. 305, E), 6.486)

Scripture also teaches this correlation between dead humans (demons) and the gods of the various nations. Arnold has well written:

"These idols, however, were not mere harmless stone images a covenant person could be indifferent to. There was a real spiritual dimension to the pagan cults and the worship of idols. Biblical writers complete the picture of Yahweh's attitude toward false gods by portraying the pagan cults as the work of demons. In Deuteronomy 32:16-17, Israel's abandonment of God for idols in the wilderness is explicitly described: They made him jealous with their foreign gods and angered him with their detestable idols. They sacrificed to demons, which are not God-gods they had not known, gods that recently appeared, gods your fathers did not fear. (italics mine) The Psalms express the same thought. One psalm describes Israel's entry into Canaan, deploring the fact that God's people had adopted many of the local customs and had worshiped the local idols. They also "sacrificed their sons and their daughters to demons," which the psalmist sets parallel with the statement that they "sacrificed to the idols of Canaan" (Ps 106:37-38). In Psalm 96:5, where the Hebrew text reads, "for all the gods of the nations are idols," the Septuagint text (the Greek translation) reads, "for all the gods of the nations are demons." The Septuagint reflects the Jewish conviction that pagan religions had a close affiliation with the demonic realm. This belief also became the conviction of the apostle Paul (1 Cor 10:19-21)." (Clinton E. Arnold, Powers of Darkness: Principalities & Powers in Paul's Letters, 56-57 (Kindle Edition); Downers Grove, Illinois; InterVarsity Press)

Thus, it is very likely that Odin was indeed Woden, a human being worshipped by his descendants as a demon after his death!

Odin Is Not Eternal

Regardless of whether or not Odin was a deified human being, the Norse scriptures are clear that Odin was not the original Creator, nor does he posses the qualities of being eternal (especially since he will one day be destroyed).

Speaking of Odin from the Norse scriptures, Lindow notes:

"God of poetry, wisdom, hosts, and the dead; in the received mythology head of the pantheon. Odin's father was Bur, son of Búri, the form licked from the salt blocks by the proto-cow Audhumla. Odin's mother was Bestla, a giantess, the daughter of Bölthorn. His very genealogy, therefore, replicates a basic operational pattern, namely, that the gods take as wives (or make children with) the females of the giant group….

"At Ragnorak Fenrir will run free and will destroy Odin, only to have vengeance taken on him by Vidar. The cosmos
44

will reemerge from teh fires and chaos of Ragnorok, but Odin will not be there." (John Lindow, Norse Mythology: A Guide to Gods, Heroes, Rituals, and Beliefs, 247-251 (Kindle Edition); New York, NY; oxford University Press)

Please notice that even the Norse scriptures themselves acknowledge that Odin is not the eternal Creator of the universe.

Since Odin is not the true Creator, then he is not worthy of worship.

> "However, just like any other finite thing, a finite god would need a cause. Also, it seems that an imperfect god would not be worthy of worship. A perfect and infinite God, however, does not have these problems and is able to overcome evil since He has both the desire and the ability to do it...
>
> "If the gods are not eternal, but come from nature, then they are not the ultimate. Why worship something that is not of ultimate value? It would be better to worship nature itself which gave the gods birth; however, that would be pantheism...
>
> "There is also a problem with the notion of an eternal universe." (Norman L. Geisler & Ronald M. Brooks, When Skeptics Ask: A Handbook on Christian Evidences, 53 (Kindle Edition); Grand Rapids, Michigan; Baker Books)

Norse scriptures are clear that their gods are not truly Divine.

They had a beginning, and they will have an end.

Proof

Christians are commanded to provide rational evidence for why we believe what we do:

> *1 Peter 3:15—But sanctify the Lord God in your hearts, and always be ready to give a defense to everyone who asks you a reason for the hope that is in you, with meekness and fear;*

The word "defense" speaks to us about a rational defense.

"The word was often used of the argument for the defense in a court of law, and though the word may have the idea of a judicial interrogation in which one is called to answer for the manner in which he has exercised his responsibility (Beare), the word can also mean an informal explanation or defense of one's position. The word would aptly describe giving an answer to the skeptical, abusive, or derisive inquiries of ill-disposed neighbors (Kelly) (Cleon Rogers II and III, The New Linguistic And Exegetical Key To The Greek New Testament, 575; Grand Rapids, Michigan, Zondervan Publishing House)."

When we ask for proof regarding the teachings of the Norse religion, is there any to be had?

Archaeology

Where is the evidence that any of these the accounts in the Eddas actually took place?

From a historical point of view, there are no discernible miracles that Odin or the Norse pantheon performed which may be examined and documented by credible sources. More to the point, while there are many accounts of journeys to the heavenly realms, there is not any discernible evidence that the Norse scriptures are historically verifiable.

Contrast this with the Bible, which accounts (including its' miraculous accounts) have been continually confirmed by archaeology:

> "W. F. Albright of Johns Hopkins University states, "There can be no doubt that archaeology has confirmed the substantial historicity of Old Testament tradition." Likewise, Millar Burrows of Yale University offers this endorsement: On the whole, however, archaeological work has unquestionably strengthened confidence in the reliability of the scriptural record. More than one archaeologist has found his respect for the Bible increased by the experience of excavation in Palestine. Archaeology has in many cases refuted the views of modern critics. It has shown, in a number of instances, that these views rest on

46

false assumptions and unreal, artificial schemes of historical development. This is a real contribution and not to be minimized.'" (Paul E. Little, *Know Why You Believe,* 108 (Kindle Edition); Downers Grove, Illinois; InterVarsity Press)

Kennedy, in discussing numerous ways that archaeology has helped to confirm the Bible, has noted:

"Artifacts related to the Bible specifically have illuminated or confirmed events, chronologies, practices, terminology, locations, and individuals that would otherwise have remained a mystery. As an example, there are currently about 70 individuals mentioned in the Old Testament who have been confirmed by archaeological artifacts, and about 32 individuals in the New Testament so far confirmed by archaeology, with several more people from the Bible tentatively identified by archaeological artifacts. Many artifacts have also illuminated obscure words and practices in the Bible, from times long ago in lands far away, that would be misunderstood or unknown otherwise....

"The fallacious arguments claiming that the archaeological data shows the Bible to be unhistorical myth, legend, or propaganda are demonstrated to be sensationalism and falsehood by the artifact evidence presented in this book. Although 101 objects were presented, there might have been around 500 artifacts noted if there were no space restrictions and the scope was more comprehensive! Further, every year new and significant discoveries connected to the Bible are being made, suggesting that the amount of archaeological evidence will increase as time goes on and as ancient sites are found and excavated. Pass on this information to others, visit archaeological sites and museums to see these artifacts with your own eyes, and be on the lookout for these new exciting finds, which are usually announced in press releases, archaeology journals, and documentaries. Only time will tell what else lies buried, and the mysteries that will be

revealed as more artifacts of the past are rediscovered."
(Titus M. Kennedy, Unearthing the Bible: 101
Archaeological Discoveries That Bring the Bible to Life,
238-239 (Kindle Edition); Eugene, Oregon; Harvest House
Publishers)

The differences here between Christianity and the Norse
religion are insurmountable.

Prophecy

Another powerful evidence that should be considered is in
regard to prophecy and fulfillment.

During the Old Testament period, God challenged the gods of
the pagans to prove that they were truly gods by revealing detailed
knowledge of the future before it took place.

For example:

> *Isaiah 41:21-24—"Present your case," says the LORD.
> "Bring forth your strong reasons," says the King of Jacob.
> (22) "Let them bring forth and show us what will happen;
> Let them show the former things, what they were, That we
> may consider them, And know the latter end of them; Or
> declare to us things to come. (23) Show the things that are
> to come hereafter, That we may know that you are gods; Yes,
> do good or do evil, That we may be dismayed and see it
> together. (24) Indeed you are nothing, And your work is
> nothing; He who chooses you is an abomination.*

> *Isaiah 42:9—Behold, the former things have come to pass,
> And new things I declare; Before they spring forth I tell you
> of them.*

> *Isaiah 44:6-7— Thus says the LORD, the King of Israel, And
> his Redeemer, the LORD of hosts: I am the First and I am the
> Last; Besides Me there is no God. (7) And who can proclaim
> as I do? Then let him declare it and set it in order for Me,
> Since I appointed the ancient people. And the things that are
> coming and shall come, Let them show these to them.*

Isaiah 45:21—Tell and bring forth your case; Yes, let them take counsel together. Who has declared this from ancient time? Who has told it from that time? Have not I, the LORD? And there is no other God besides Me, A just God and a Savior; There is none besides Me.

True prophecy, of course, must meet obvious standards.

One author has described such:

"First, though, let us remind ourselves of several principles that govern the validity of genuine prophecy. (1) True prophecies are stated emphatically; they are not couched in the jargon of contingency (unless, of course, contextual evidence suggests that one is dealing with a conditional prophecy). (2) Generally, a significant time frame must lapse between the prophetic utterance and the fulfillment, so as to exclude the possibility of 'educated speculation.' (3) The prophecy must involve specific details, not vague generalities. (4) The predictive declarations must be fulfilled precisely and completely. No mere substantial percentage will suffice. One should recognize, though, that occasionally a prophecy may contain figurative terminology; this does not, however, militate against its evidential validity." (Wayne Jackson, 'Babylon: A Test Case In Prophecy,' in Kyle Butt, *Behold! The Word Of God*, 1598-1604 (Kindle Edition); Montgomery, Alabama; Apologetics Press)

Now, the Bible has hundreds of examples of amazingly complex prophecies which were written long before their fulfillment. Hundreds of examples of this may be found in what is known as Messianic prophecies (i.e., prophecies made in the Old Testament period from about 1450 B.C. To 408 B.C.). These prophecies describe in shocking detail the details and characteristics of Jesus Christ, literally written over a thousand years before He was born into the world!

"In the Old Testament, there are sixty major messianic prophecies and approximately 270 ramifications that were fulfilled in one person, Jesus Christ. It is helpful to look at all these predictions fulfilled in Christ as His "address." You've probably never realize how important the details of *your* name and address are-and yet these details set you apart from the five billion other people who also inhabit this planet. With even greater detail, God wrote an address in history to single out His Son, the Messiah, the Savior of mankind, from anyone who has ever lived in history-past, present, or future. The specifics of this address can be found in the Old Testament, a document written over a period of a thousand years, which contains more than three hundred references to His coming. Using the science of probability, we find the chances of just forty-eight of these prophecies being fulfilled in one person to be right at one in 10^{157} (a one followed by 157 zeros!)...The following probabilities are taken from that book (Peter Stoner, *Science Speaks,* M.T.) to show that coincidence is ruled out by the science of probability. Stoner says that by using the modern science of probability in reference to just eight prophecies, "we find that the chance that any man might have lived down to the present time and fulfilled all eight prophecies is 1 in 10^{17}." That would be 1 in 100, 000, 000, 000, 000, 000, 000. In order to help us comprehend this staggering probability, Stoner illustrates it by supposing that..."we take 10^{17} silver dollars and lay them on the face of Texas. They will cover all of the state two feet deep. Now mark one of these silver dollars and stir the whole mass thoroughly, all over the state. Blindfold a man and tell him that he can travel as far as he wishes, but he must pick up one silver dollar and say that this is the right one. What chance would have of getting the right one? Just the same chance that the prophets would have had of writing these eight prophecies and having them all come true in any one man, from their day to the present time, providing they wrote in their own wisdom. Now these prophecies were either given by the inspiration of God or the prophets just wrote them as they thought they should be. In such a case the prophets had just one chance in 10^{17} of having them come true in any man, but they all came true in Christ. This means that the fulfillment of these eight prophecies alone proves that God inspired the writing of these prophecies to a definiteness which lacks only one chance in 10^{17} of being absolute." (Josh McDowell and Bill Wilson, *A Ready Defense: The Best Of Josh McDowell*, 210, 213 (Kindle Edition); Nashville, TN: Thomas Nelson Publishers)

Now, how do the Norse scriptures compare with this kind of evidence?

According to the Norse scriptures, it is Odin's wife, Frigg, who has the gift of prophecy.

However, she refuses to use her alleged gift of prophecy!

"Frigg is his wife, and she knows all the fates of men, though she speaks no prophecy,--as is said here, when Odin himself spake with him of the Æsir whom men call Loki: Thou art mad now, | Loki, and reft of mind,—Why, Loki, leav'st thou not off? Frigg, methinks, | is wise in all fates, Though herself say them not!" (Snorri Sturlson, Prose Edda (Translated by Arthur Gilchrist Brodeur),), 25 (Kindle Edition))

Did Christianity Steal Norse Religious Belief?

One of the most often made claims today is that Christians "ripped off" various elements of pagan religion and incorporated them into Christianity. This is often known as the "copycat theory."

A study of the Eddas (along with these conspiracy claims) clearly refutes such charges. One reason for this is because the religious teachings of the Eddas clearly were written nearly a thousand years after the New Testament Scriptures! As such, if any copycatting took place, it was undoubtedly the Eddas borrowing from the Old and New Testament Scriptures!

"The hypothesis is faced by one obvious difficulty. The difficulty appears in the late date of most of the sources of information...Every step is uncertain. In the first place, it is often by no means clear that the pagan usage has not been influenced by Christianity. The Church did not long remain obscure; even early in the second century, according to the testimony of Pliny, it was causing the heathen temples to be deserted. What is more likely than that in an age of syncretism the adherents of pagan religion should borrow weapons from so successful a rival? It must be remembered that the paganism of the Hellenistic age had elevated syncretism to a system; it had absolutely no objection of principle against receiving elements from every source. In the Christian Church, on the other hand, there was a strong objection to such procedure; Christianity from the beginning was like Judaism in being exclusive. It regarded with the utmost abhorrence anything that was tainted by a pagan origin. This abhorrence, at least in the early period, more than overbalanced the fact that the Christians for the most part had formerly been pagans, so that it might be thought natural for them to retain something of pagan belief. Conversion involved a passionate renunciation of former beliefs. Such, at any rate, was clearly the kind of conversion that was required by Paul." (John Machen, *The Origin Of Paul's Religion,* 3715-3740 (Kindle Edition).

Another researcher, discussing the popular and factually erroneous movie known as Zeitgeist (which strongly advocates the copycat theory), describes some of the fallacies with the copycat theory:

> "Space constraints preclude a discussion of all but a few of the many specific fallacies Zeitgeist commits. One of the most blatant is the terminology fallacy. That is, events in the lives of the mythical gods, for example, are expressed using Christian terminology in order subtly to manipulate viewers into accepting that the same events in the life of Jesus also happened in the lives of mythical gods. We are told, for instance, that Horus, Krishna, Dionysius, and others were "baptized," "born of a virgin," "crucified," and "resurrected"—just to mention a few. Examples of such locutions, however, involve assertions with no evidence, are ripped out of their Christian context, or are obtained from

post-first-century sources. Nash observes: "One frequently encounters scholars who first use Christian terminology to describe pagan beliefs and practices and then marvel at the awesome parallels that they think they have discovered." A few examples will suffice. It is claimed that Horus was "born of the virgin Isis-Meri." In the most common version of the Osiris-Isis-Horus myth, Osiris has been murdered by Set and cut into 14 pieces. Isis, his wife (so we can assume she is not a virgin), retrieves all but one of the pieces and reconstructs Osiris. She cannot find the fourteenth piece (his sexual organ); so she fashions one out of wood and then has sexual relations with him. She later gives birth to Horus. Here are other alleged "virgin births." Attis is conceived when Zeus spilled his seed on the side of a mountain which eventually became a pomegranate tree. Nana, mother of Attis, is sitting under the tree when a pomegranate falls in her lap and she becomes pregnant with the child of Zeus. Devaki, the mother of Krishna, had seven children before Krishna. Dionysius's mother, Semele, was impregnated by Zeus. In fact, none of the mythical gods experienced a "virginal" conception even close to the manner that Scripture claims of Jesus. What of the claim that these figures were "crucified"? Krishna was shot in the foot with an arrow and died from his wounds. Attis castrated himself in a jealous rage, fled into the wilderness, and died. Depending on which version of the myth one reads, Horus either (1) did not die, (2) was merely stung by a scorpion, or (3) his death is conflated with the death of Osiris. Adonis was gored by a wild boar. Yet, Acharya S justifies the use of the term "crucify" to describe the death of Horus as follows: When it is asserted that Horus (or Osiris) was "crucified" it should be kept in mind that it was not part of the Horus/ Osiris myth that the murdered god was held down and nailed on a cross, as we perceive the meaning of "crucified" to be, based on the drama we believe allegedly took place during Christ's purported passion. Rather in one myth Osiris is torn to pieces before being raised from the dead, while Horus is stung by a scorpion prior to his resurrection. However, Egyptian deities, including Horus, were depicted in cruciform with arms extended or outstretched, as in various images that are comparable to crucifixes. So, according to Murdock, anytime deities are depicted with arms outstretched, we are justified in claiming they were crucified. A final example is the claim that all of these gods were "resurrected" from the dead. While the idea that the resurrection of Jesus was borrowed from the "dying and rising gods" of the pagan mystery religions was very popular at one time, almost all scholars have abandoned this view today. Jonathan Z. Smith writes: All of the deities that have been identified as belonging to the class of dying and rising deities can be subsumed under the two larger classes of disappearing deities or dying deities. In the first case, the deities return but have not died; in the second case, the gods die but do not return. There is no unambiguous instance in the history of religions of a dying and rising deity. The best known example of a resurrection claim is the Horus/Osiris myth, but Osiris did not rise from the dead and return to this world as did Jesus. Instead, he was made king of the underworld. After his death, Attis eventually turns into a pine tree. Many sources claiming resurrections were written long after the first-century sources for Christianity and therefore could not have influenced the Gospel accounts or Paul's teaching in letters such as 1 Corinthians. A second-century source tells us of the resurrection of Adonis. Claims of Krishna's resurrection do not emerge until the sixth or seventh century. Older tradition holds he simply entered the spirit world where he is always present. This is not a resurrection in the manner in which the Gospels claim Jesus rose from the dead. A second fallacy is the nonbiblical fallacy. This is where a parallel is claimed about some aspect of Jesus that is not even reported in the Gospel accounts. One example is where Zeitgeist claims a parallel between the three stars in the belt of Orion called the "three kings" and the three kings who visited the baby Jesus. The problem is that the Gospels never call them kings and never state how many there are. Another example, mentioned above, is the oft-claimed parallel of the birth date of all these deities, December 25, with the birth date of Christ. A third fallacy is the chronological fallacy. In order for the copycat charge of borrowing to succeed, one needs to provide evidence that the parallel preceded the writing of the Gospel accounts and the letters of Paul—all written in the first century. However, this simply is not the case. First, as mentioned above, there is no evidence that there was any pagan mystery influence in first-century Palestine. Second, the mystery religions evolved over time, and as they did, their beliefs and narratives changed. This results in several versions of the various pagan myths. Most of the evidence we have of their narratives comes from sources dated in the second and third centuries, a time when they were experiencing the peak of their influence in the Mediterranean world. We have little evidence of the beliefs of these religions from the first century. Nash comments: Far too many writers on the subject use the available sources to form the plausible reconstructions of the third-century mystery experience and then uncritically reason back to what they think must have been the earlier nature of the cults. We have plenty of information about the mystery religions of the third century. But important differences exist between these religions and earlier expressions of the mystery experience (for which adequate information is extremely slim). A fourth fallacy closely connected with this last one is the source fallacy. One of the comments often made in praise of Zeitgeist is how well the claims are documented. It is true that, in the transcript of the movie, many of the claims are documented; some by multiple sources. The brief section quoted above has 44 citations from 11 different sources to support its claims. At first glance this may seem impressive. As scholars will insist, however, it is not the number of sources that matter but their quality—and the quality of these sources is highly questionable. Not one of them is a primary source of the religion under discussion. They are all secondary, and most of them are the older, discredited sources that have been abandoned by most critical scholars. These sources often make undocumented assertions, speculate on causal relationships, and offer selective interpretations of some texts (of which there is much unrevealed disagreement). Often the authors are not experts in the field of religion, or they are experts in a related field (such as Egyptology), neither of which is a qualification over which to drape a cloak of scholarship. What inevitably results is rabid and unprincipled speculation on the origin of Christianity. One reason why primary sources are not relevant is that they are not as conclusive as copycat theorists would lead one to believe. Because these ancient religions evolved over time, often no one authoritative story exists to which one may appeal. For example, the story of Horus in Zeitgeist is pieced together from a number of sources, some of which conflict. It is like playing "connect the dots," but interpreting how to connect those dots is a slippery, unscholarly enterprise. These writers seem to use the life of Jesus as a guide for how to connect the dots for the life of Horus and then proclaim that the story of Jesus is based on Horus—when actually it is the other way around! Other religions don't fare much better. For example, there is no text for Mithraism; everything we know about the religion comes either from interpreting reliefs and statues or from brief comments by other ancient writers, almost all of whom are post-first century. Metzger comments, "It goes without saying that alleged parallels which are discovered by pursuing such methodology evaporate when they are confronted with the original texts. In a word, one must beware of what have been called 'parallels made plausible by selective description.'" The final fallacy to mention is the difference fallacy, which is committed by an overemphasis on (supposed) similarities between two things while ignoring the vast and relevant differences between them. Again, Metzger observes, "In arriving at a just estimate of the relation of the Mysteries to Christianity as reflected in the New Testament, attention must be given to their differences as well as resemblances." The differences between Christianity and the pagan religions are enormous, and yet Zeitgeist ignores them. Here are a few examples. First, whereas all of the mystery religions are tied into the vegetative cycle of birth-death-rebirth and continue to follow this cycle year after year ad infinitum, Christianity is linear, viewing all of history as headed on a trajectory culminating in God's transforming this world into a renewed creation—the new heaven and new earth. Second, mystery religions are secretive. One has to go through secret initiation rites to become a member. They are full of secret knowledge, available only to some, which is one reason we don't know a lot about them. By contrast, Christianity is open to all to scrutinize and to embrace. It is a "mystery of revelation." Third, doctrine and beliefs are totally unimportant in pagan mystery religions. In fact, a characteristic hallmark is their syncretism: you can hold almost any belief and still become a member of their religion. They emphasize feeling and experience over doctrine and belief. In diametric contrast, doctrine and beliefs are the heart and soul of Christianity, which is highly exclusivistic. That is one of the major reasons Christians were so persecuted in the Roman Empire. They held that there was only one way to God. Fourth, the pagan mystery religions are almost completely void of almost any ethical element. Rahner comments: At no stage [of their development] do the mysteries bear comparison with the ethical commandments of the new Testaments and their realization in early Christianity. The two terms are truly incommensurable—and this is not the foregone conclusion of apologists but results from an unbiased examination of the sources by scholars who cannot be accused of denominational commitment. Fifth, even if one accepts the "dying and rising gods" concept, the meaning of the death of Christ is completely different. Christ died for the sins of mankind; none of the pagan gods died for someone else. Pagan gods died under compulsion, but Jesus died willingly. Jesus died and was raised once; the pagan gods die cyclically. Jesus' death was not tragic or a defeat; it was a victory. Pagans mourn and lament the death of their gods. Finally, and most importantly, the view of the church from the very beginning is that Jesus was a real person who lived in history. His death and resurrection were actual events of history. Metzger states, "Unlike the deities of the Mysteries, who were nebulous figures of an imaginary past, the Divine being whom the Christian worshipped as Lord was known as a real Person on earth only a short time before the earliest documents of the New Testament were written." It is the historicity of Jesus' life, death, and resurrection that makes Christianity the true anti-mystery." (Mark Foreman,' Challenging The Zeitgeist Movie: Parallelomania On Steroids, in Paul Copan & William Lane Craig, Come Let Us Reason: New Essays In Christian Apologetics, 3509-3615 (Kindle Edition); Nashville, TN: B&H Publishing Group)

The Foreshadowing Of The Gospel In Norse Mythology

Finally, it is worth considering that there are elements of Norse religion which may reflect hope in the Good News of Jesus Christ.

One of the oldest prophecies in the Bible is found in the Book of Genesis:

> *Genesis 3:15—And I will put enmity Between you and the woman, And between your seed and her Seed; He shall bruise your head, And you shall bruise His heel."*

One researcher, Lois Clymer, traces how the fragments of this prophecy of Jesus Christ are interwoven throughout the various religions of the world:

> "Can we prove that Christianity was not borrowed from pagan myths and mysteries? We can, by tracing the fascinating threads which show the story, the Sacred Promise, woven throughout history. The story of Jesus begins not in Bethlehem but at the beginning of man's time on Earth. Some of these threads are the myths, the constellations of the zodiac, and other astronomical signs."

(Lois Clymer, Sacred Strands: The Story Of A Redeemer Woven Throughout History, 7 (Kindle Edition); Sisters, Oregon; Deep River Books)

Regarding the Norse religion, she documents:

"Viking" and "Norse" are two words that can be used interchangeably. They refer to the Indo-European people who lived in Scandinavia during the Viking Age. The different names may refer somewhat to their different lifestyles. The Norse were traders, whereas the Vikings were primarily farmers who were sometimes pirates and warriors who traveled in their longboats to faraway parts of the world, to trade and sometimes to conquer other lands in order to expand their territory and to settle. The Viking raiders were made up of landowners, freemen, and any adventuresome young clan members who were looking for booty overseas. At home they were farmers, but at sea they were raiders and pillagers. They raided and colonized wide areas of Europe from the seventh to eleventh centuries. Their burning, plundering, and killing earned them the name "Viking," which means "pirate" in the early Scandinavian languages. Most of what is known about the origin of the Norse and Viking people is derived from the evidence of language. The Germanic languages include English, Norweigian, Swedish, Danish, Dutch, and German. Various Germanic tribes migrated into Italy, Gaul, Spain, and North Africa. Many merged with other people groups such as the Danes in Denmark, the Swedes in Sweden, and the Saxons in England. Tacitus was a senator and a historian of the Roman Empire. He wrote and published a book now known as the Germania in 98 AD. He told that the Germans were sheep and cattle farmers and that most of their food came from milk, cheese, and meat, but that they also grew grain, root crops, and vegetables. According to most historians, the fall of the Roman Empire in 476 AD resulted from the successful attempt of the Germanic people to occupy the lands of the Roman Empire. The eastern Germanic people remained migratory for a longer period of time, whereas the western Germanic people were more settled, with an agricultural base which allowed them to support more people. They periodically cleared forest land to extend their agriculture. The Germanic people created a strong military and were fierce in battle. Their love of battle appeared to be linked with their religion; two of their most important gods, Odin (also called Woden) and his son Thor were gods of war. The leaders of the clans were called chieftains, and one of their responsibilities was to keep the warriors united. The Vikings terrorized Europe between 700 AD and 1100 AD. The Viking navigators used the sun and stars to guide them. They also relied on landmarks such as islands. When they invaded a new territory, they usually came with a few hundred ships and thousands of warriors. They were known for their surprise attacks. They could row their light boats into shallow rivers. They fought with axes and used both hands to swing their axes at enemies. The Vikings 'skills in sailing and shipmaking gave them the ability to travel farther and faster than most sailors of their time. Their fast, low-draft longship had an average length of one hundred feet with a width of twenty-five feet, could carry two hundred armed men with fifty oars, and could sometimes achieve speeds of eleven knots (more than twelve miles per hour). When the areas they had conquered converted to Christianity, the Old Norse values were weakened. Many of the Norse and Vikings eventually became part of the cultures they had come in contact with. The Danish Vikings who invaded England became part of the English culture, while those who settled Normandy became French. Earliest History The Genesis writer identifies where the sixteen grandsons of Noah repopulated after the flood. It is easy to find these sixteen places because people in various areas often called themselves by the name of their common ancestor and also sometimes named their land, major rivers, and major cities by his name. In addition, they sometimes claimed their ancestor as their god. All sixteen grandsons can be traced to Europe, Asia, and Africa. Two of the grandsons, Gomer and Tiras, both sons of Japheth, can be traced to the Germans and to the Vikings. The Bible says Gomer settled in the "north quarters." The Gauls in the first century were called Gomerites, and the Welsh language itself has been called Gomeraeg. One of the sons of Gomer was Ashkenaz, which is the Hebrew word for Germany. Josephus wrote that Tiras, another grandson of Noah, became the ancestor of the Thirsians (Thracians). Tiras was worshipped by his descendants as Thuras (Thor), the god of thunder. The basic dress of the Thracian and Viking warriors was a tunic, a cloak or cape, a cap, and boots. The cloak or cape was thrown over one shoulder. They carried a shield and spear, plus a small sword or dagger. Thor Thor, the son of Odin, was the god of thunder and of the sky in Norse and old Germanic mythology. The thunder god is known for his chief weapon, the mighty hammer Mjellnir or Crusher, which returned magically to his hand like a boomerang when he threw it. His hammer caused lightning which flashed across the sky when he used it. Thor also wore a magical belt that doubled his strength, and he owned a pair of goats that pulled his chariot across the sky. Hymir was the father of the god Tyr. Hymir owned a large kettle, and Tyr and Thor paid Hymir a visit to get this kettle. During that visit Thor and Hymir went fishing, using an ox for bait. Something bit the ox, and when Thor drew up his line he realized that he had hooked Jormungand, the giant serpent. Putting his feet on the ocean floor, Thor pulled and pulled on the line while the serpent spit out poison. Just as Thor was about to strike the serpent with his hammer, Hymir cut the line and the serpent sank back down. The myths say they will fight again on the day called Ragnarok, the end of the world. At that day, Thor will kill the serpent but will die from its poison. Again, we see in this myth a type of the battle described in Genesis 3:15. Thor struggles with the serpent and will eventually kill it, even though he will die from its poison. In Genesis the man born of a woman conquers the serpent, even though he is bruised by this serpent. The thread of the Redeemer continues to appear throughout the globe." (Lois Clymer, Sacred Strands: The

Story Of A Redeemer Woven Through History, 69-71
(Kindle Edition); Sisters, Oregon; Deep River Books)

The grace of the Lord Jesus Christ, and the love of God, and the communion of the Holy Spirit, be with you all. Amen.

Questions

1. Who are the three main gods of the Norse pantheon?

   _____

2. What is the "copycat theory?"

   _____

   _____

3. Who was Euhermerus and what his theory of the origins of the pagan gods and goddesses ?

   _____

   _____

   _____

4. Who are some other early writers who confirm Euhermerus's theory?

   _____

   _____

   _____

5. What are the main scriptures of the Norse religion?

   _____

   _____

6. "In the Old Testament, there are _____ major messianic prophecies and approximately _____ ramifications that were fulfilled in one person, _____ _____ It is helpful to look at all these predictions fulfilled in Christ as His "address."....The specifics of this address can be found in the Old Testament, a document written over a period of a thousand years, which contains more than _____ _____ references to His coming. Using the science of probability, we find the chances of just forty-eight of these prophecies being fulfilled in one person to be

right at one in 10^{157} (a one followed by 157 zeros!)...The following probabilities are taken from that book (Peter Stoner, *Science Speaks,* M.T.) to show that coincidence is ruled out by the science of probability. Stoner says that by using the modern science of probability in reference to just eight prophecies, "we find that the chance that any man might have lived down to the present time and fulfilled all eight prophecies is 1 in 10^{17}." That would be 1 in 100, 000, 000, 000, 000, 000, 000. In order to help us comprehend this staggering probability, Stoner illustrates it by supposing that..."we take 10^{17}silver dollars and lay them on the face of Texas. They will cover all of the state two feet deep. Now mark _____ of these silver dollars and stir the whole mass thoroughly, all over the _____. Blindfold a man and tell him that he can travel as far as he wishes, but he must pick up one silver dollar and say that this is the right one. What chance would have of getting the _____ one? Just the same chance that the prophets would have had of writing these eight prophecies and having them all come true in any one man, from their day to the present time, providing they wrote in their own wisdom....This means that the _____ of these _____ prophecies alone proves that God inspired the writing of these prophecies to a definiteness which lacks only one chance in 10^{17} of being absolute." (Josh McDowell and Bill Wilson, *A Ready Defense: The Best Of Josh McDowell,* 210, 213 (Kindle Edition); Nashville, TN: Thomas Nelson Publishers)

7. Describe the nine realms.

_____
_____
_____
_____
_____
_____
_____

8. According to the Norse scriptures, is Odin an eternal god?

_____

9. Who are the Nephilim, and who in the Norse scriptures has an interesting connection with them?

_____

_____

_____

_____

10. What are some problems with the copycat theory?

_____

_____

_____

_____

_____

_____

_____

11. According to the Prose Edda, _____ had the gift of prophecy but refused to use it.

Lesson Three

Norse Paganism (Two)

In this lesson, we will further consider Norse beliefs.

We will also examine some evidence which connects Odin (the chief god of the Norse pantheon) with the demonic beings described in the Holy Bible as the Nephilim.

The Three Most Famous Stories Of Odin

Within the Eddas, there are three stories of Odin which are particularly well-known.

1. Odin's Gaining The Mead Of Poetry;

2. Odin's Sacrifice Of One Of His Eyes To Gain Wisdom From The Well Of Mimir;

3. Odin's Hanging Himself On The Worldtree To Gain The Runes

These three are perhaps the most well-known in Odinist scripture because it is believed that Odin then communicated the knowledge of these gifts to mankind.

Let's examine each of these stories.

Acquiring The Mead Of Poetry

Odinists believe that there is a certain type of power inherent in words. As a result, words uttered in chant or rhyme may have abilities to transform reality in various ways.

One author describes the mead of poetry:

> "After the first war, when the Æsir and Vanir tribes made peace, the gods collectively spat into a massive cauldron and derived a being from the mixture; his name was Kvasir. He

was so wise that there was no question he couldn't provide a suitable answer to. Because of this gift, he wandered the realms, dispensing his wisdom and answering the questions of those he met. He followed that path until he ran into two dwarves named Fjalarr and Galarr (meaning 'deceiver 'and 'screamer'), who killed him and drained his blood. They mixed his blood with honey to create the mead of poetry, which they poured into three containers: two vats called Sodn and Bodn and a pot called Óðrerir, which the mead would assume the name of. Following the creation of Óðrerir, a Jötun named Gilling and his wife visited the dwarves. In short, Fjalarr and Galarr killed them both, which resulted in their son, Suttangr, coming to the dwelling of the dwarves and torturing them. He put them on a small, rocky reef-island below sea level until they begged for their lives. Suttangr took the mead of poetry and then stored the three containers in a mountain called Hnitbjörg under the protection of his daughter, Gunnloð. Either because Kvasir didn't return to Ásgarðr for an extended period of time, or because Óðinn saw the events from his throne, he desired the mead of poetry. He travelled to Jǫtunheimr under the name Bǫlverkr (literally "evil-doer") and came by a group of nine workers, mowing a field with scythes. Bǫlverkr had a brilliant whetstone in his pocket, which he used to sharpen one of their scythes. The workers were all so impressed that they wondered what he would trade for the stone. Bǫlverkr said the last man standing could have it, after which he threw the whetstone into the air, watched the workers kill each other, caught the stone and carried on his way. Bǫlverkr came to the house of the brother of Suttangr, Baugi. He announced that Baugi had lost nine workers in the field and suggested that he would do the work of nine men for the summer, under the condition that Baugi would help him secure a drink of the mead of poetry. Baugi agreed to the terms, and Óðinn did the work of nine men for the summer. After that, Baugi went to his brother, Suttangr and asked if he would share any of the mead with his new farmhand, Bǫlverkr, but Suttangr refused to give a drop away. Upon hearing that, Oðinn came up with another plan. He got out a drill known as Rati and instructed Baugi to bore into the mountain, Hnitbjörg. When Baugi said the deed was done, Oðinn blew into the hole but a bit of rock flew back at him; he realized then that Baugi was trying to betray him. He told Baugi to keep drilling, and once the chamber was visible, Oðinn turned himself into a snake and slithered through the hole as Baugi tried to stab him. When Oðinn made his way into the chamber (probably disguising himself as a more handsome man), he seduced Gunnloð and she agreed to give him three drinks of the mead in exchange for spending three nights with her. On the third night, Oðinn took his three drinks of mead and on each drink, he consumed an entire container. Oðinn then turned himself into an eagle and flew out of the mountain, headed back to Ásgarðr. As Oðinn flew through the air, he didn't realise Suttangr had also turned into an eagle and was close behind him. When Oðinn looked back, he was startled so he defecated some of the mead into Suttangr's face. That mead is for bad poets. When Oðinn returned to Ásgarðr, he regurgitated the rest of the mead into a large cauldron, and it was then shared it with gods and humans. In the poem Hávamál, Suttangr came to Ásgarðr searching for a man named Bǫlverkr, to which Oðinn responds, "Well, he's not here." Oðinn follows up with the famous St. 110 of Hávamál, "I believe that Oðinn swore an oath to them-but who can trust Oðinn? He left Suttangr deceived in his own home, and he left Gunnloð weeping."" (Ingvar Askelson, Norse Gods and Goddesses: Guide To Understanding Scandinavian Deities And The Viking Religion, 11-13 (Kindle Edition); NeoViking Co. Lulu Press Self-Publishing Company)

The story of the mead of poetry ties in with the next two stories, and is intimately connected to the Norse belief in magic.

The Sacrifice Of Odin's Eye

Mimir is the name of a wise god from whom Odin learned nine spells. It is declared that he was once a full-bodied man that was decapitated. Being desirous of the occult knowledge of Mimir, Odin retained control over Mimir's head. Using magic spells and various potions, Odin kept the head preserved and used it to speak with the dead. Later, the head of Mimir was deposited into a well. Sometime after this, Odin plucked out one of his eyes (it is not declared which one) and sacrificed it for further occult knowledge at the Well Of Mimir.

The Sacrifice Of Odin On The Worldtree

Perhaps the most well-known story of Odin from the Eddas regards his sacrifice on the Worldtree. For nine days, Odin willingly hangs himself from the Worldtree. He is even impaled by his own weapon, the spear Gungnir! It is while in this state (half-choked, losing blood, semiconscious) that he is able to gain understanding into the runes.

In Norse mythology, runes are symbols that many believe contain magical powers to influence the world of man. The word "rune" comes from the Norse *runa,* which meant "a secret" or "to whisper."

Writing of the Asatru belief that runes are imbued with magical power, one author writes:

> "But how could such a procedure possibly work? The traditional Norse answer would be that in the Web of Wyrd (fate, destiny), all things and events resonate in a profound and luminous way and that Runes faithfully record the signature of the energy movements underlying our own unique fate path at the moment of consultation....In the ancient world, divination was, of course, attributed to the activity of gods and spirits...How exactly do the Runes embody the wisdom of Odin? First, the runic signs carry many meanings. Each rune has a field of associations partially preserved for us in three ancient "Rune poems,"

which appear to be based on far older, oral traditions. In Norse myth, Odin was the god and patron of the oral tradition, so the wisdom of the Runes and the accumulated folk ways they represent can be seen as flowing from him and from various guises of the Goddess, from whose springs of knowledge Odin himself drew. For example, the image of the first rune, (fehu), is cattle. The primary correspondences are assets, wealth, and gain, for in ancient Norse culture you were worth as much as your herd of cattle. In a Rune reading, each rune is interpreted as an omen of personal significance—thus fehu signifies material luck and gain and is titled Abundance in this book. Obviously, we would be cheered by the appearance of fehu in a reading for the present or near future! Yet, as will be seen in part 2 of this book, "Runestaves," fehu's association with wealth, good fortune, and greed evoke far deeper mythical and legendary themes in traditional runelore. Runes can teach us self-mastery and gift us with its fruits. In the original sources, they are praised as a guide to action, a remedy for misfortune, and a magical tool for promoting empowerment, fulfillment, prosperity, and peace. This is the spirit in which the Runes function for us today." (Paul Rhys Mountfort, Nordic Runes: Understanding, Casting, and Interpreting the Ancient Viking Oracle, 7-8 (Kindle Edition); Rochester, Vermont; Destiny Books)

With this knowledge in hand, Odin then shares the runes with mankind.

Part of the Eddas, the Havamal, contain a list of spells that Odin retained from the runes. It should be noted that the Havamal does not actually contain the procedure for casting these spells, but only what types of spells they are. There are eighteen altogether. Two are supposed to be for healing, four contain charms for victory in battle, two are said to control the elements, three are for protection, one is for talking to the dead, one is for mind control, two for gaining knowledge, and the last three are love spells.

Evaluation Of The Occultism Of Norse Beliefs

Clearly, Norse religion is linked to the practice of occultism and magic.

Historically, magic is believed to be based upon two sources: psychic energy and demonic energy.

Psychic Energy And Magic

The concept that magic may be linked to psychic energy has its' roots in the notion that the universe itself is in some way Divine. This is akin to the pantheistic religions, which teach that the universe is in some way God. This was a staple of religious belief before the time of the Flood, in the world of Noah. In Jewish Kabbalah, this is known as the Doctrine Of Emanations. It states that the original Creator of the universe emptied Himself (either partly or fully) into the Creation. Psychic energy is the result of tapping into this Source, either through spells or through the supposed evolutionary development of mankind over several lifetimes of birth, death, and reincarnation. It is believed that the higher a person incarnates up the karmic ladder, the more psychic energy he develops. As such, magic is said to be the harnessing of this primordial energy.

However, pantheism as a worldview fails the tests of logic and science. The universe cannot be God! For example, consider eternality as one area of consideration here. We know that the uncaused First Cause (i.e., God) must be eternal (having no beginning, and having no end: being fully self-sufficient):

> "Here, then, is the problem: the Universe exists; it must, in some fashion, be explained. There are but three ways to account for it. (1) It is eternal. (2) It is not eternal; rather it created itself from nothing. (3) It is not eternal; it was created by something anterior, and superior, to itself. Let us now explore these ideas. First, it is now clear scientifically that the Universe is not eternal. Jastrow declares: "… in science, as in the Bible, the World begins with an act of creation. That view has not always been held by scientists.

Only as a result of the most recent discoveries can we say with a fair degree of confidence that our Universe has not existed forever; that it began abruptly, without any apparent cause, in a blinding event that defies scientific explanation" (p. 2). The very fact that scientists attempt to assign an age to the Universe admits to its having an origin! Second, it is absurd to even suggest that matter could create itself. There is no known natural process whereby matter could, from nothing, fashion itself. Dr. George E. Davis, a physicist, has said: "No material thing can create itself" (1958, p. 71). The Universe is not self-explanatory. Third, the only remaining alternative is that the Universe was created by: (a) something that existed before it did, i.e., some eternal, uncaused Cause; (b) something superior to it, for the created cannot be superior to the Creator, and; (c) something of a different nature since the finite, dependent Universe of matter is unable to explain itself." (Wayne Jackson, Eric Lyons, Kyle Butt, Surveying The Evidence, 273-293 (Kindle Edition); Montgomery, Alabama; Apologetics Press, Inc.)

God must be eternal; yet we know that the universe is not eternal (as mathematics and science demonstrate). Therefore, the universe is not God.

Consider some other inherent problems with pantheism:

"Pantheism, as a worldview, fails to adequately explain the nature of ultimate reality, the existence of the physical universe, the relationship between God and man, and the problem of evil in the world. Consider the following consequences of this worldview. First, the pantheistic concept of ultimate reality is self-defeating. If it is the case that all reality is one and everything else is simply an illusion, then there is no difference between you, a chair, a plant, or a rock. If this is true, then you do not exist as an individual. However, for you to assert that you do not exist is self-defeating, for you would have to exist to affirm that you do not exist, which is a contradiction. Further, common sense and human experience tells you that there is a distinct difference between the milk you drink, the books that you read, and the eyes that you see with. To assert that these things are merely an illusion goes against all rational thought. Second, the pantheist view of the physical universe is contrary to known science. Pantheism teaches that the universe is eternal; however, the scientific data shows otherwise. According to the Second Law of Thermodynamics, the universe is running out of usable energy. This suggests to us that the universe is not eternal. Another problem presented by the pantheistic worldview is the idea that humans must come to realize that they are God. If God, the universe, and humans are all eternal, and eternal things do not change, then how can we come to know anything new? If we learn something new, then we change from not knowing something to knowing something, which is impossible for an eternal, unchanging being. Last, the pantheistic worldview does not adequately answer the problem of evil. According to pantheism, as man realizes his divinity, he will eliminate the ignorance of believing suffering, pain, poverty, and even death are real. However, simply denying the presence of evil in the world does not negate its existence. Pain, suffering, poverty, and death are undeniably a part of human experience. Even the pantheist who wholeheartedly denies the existence of evil deals with its presence every day. Pantheists suffer pain, heartbreak, physical ailments, and even experience death. To dismiss the presence of evil as simply an illusion is not only undeniable, but it is also unlivable. In reality, pantheists must live life in such a way as to avoid evil and to promote what is good. They believe it is better to help rather than hurt a child, to give a child water rather than poison to drink, and that loving others is better than hating them. While pantheists must live in such a way as to account for the presence of evil, ultimately, pantheism provides no justification for living morally. Why should we choose good over evil? Or do right rather than wrong? If there is no ultimate standard of knowledge, no absolute standard by which we ground our beliefs, then there is no absolute standard for meaning, morals, truth, goals, or right and wrong." (Ergun Caner & Ed Hindson, The Popular Encyclopedia of Apologetics: Surveying the Evidence for the Truth of Christianity, 387-388 (Kindle Edition); Eugene, Oregon; Harvest House Publishers).

Further, the evidence is clear that reincarnation is not a real phenomenon. Within the field of past-life studies, the name of Ian Stevenson is regarded as one of the most well-respected.

Writes one author:

"Writing in the Journal of Psychical Research in 1986, James G. Matlock observed that, "Stevenson's work is so far superior to any other in this area, and the body of evidence he has amassed is so intriguing, that the case for reincarnation rests largely upon it."" It will hardly come as a surprise that Stevenson has become a hero to believers in reincarnation all over the world. It is difficult to pick up a book or pamphlet defending reincarnation and published in the last twenty-five five years or so that does not refer admiringly to Stevenson's work. What may be surprising is that his work has been praised and some of it also published in respectable journals. Reviewing the first volume of his Cases of the Reincarnation Type, the Journal of the American Medical Association praised his "painstakingly and unemotionally collected cases from India in which the evidence is difficult to explain on any assumption other than reincarnation." Two of Stevenson's articles were published in Journal of Nervous and Mental Disease whose editor, Eugene Brody, proudly told the New York Post that he had received three or four hundred requests for reprints from scientists in every discipline. In the volume Psychic Voyages in the Time-Life series on the occult Stevenson's work is treated with great respect." (Paul Edwards, Reincarnation: A Critical Examination, 3865-3872 (Kindle Edition); Amherst, New York; Prometheus Books)

After years of research on the study of reincarnation and having investigated hundreds of cases of alleged past-life experiences, what does Stevenson conclude?

> "I would only here reiterate that I consider these cases suggestive of reincarnation and nothing more. All the cases have deficiencies as have all their reports. Neither any case individually nor all of them collectively offers anything like a proof of reincarnation. My most important single conclusion about them is of the need for further study of similar cases. If anyone takes up this task I shall consider my efforts amply rewarded." (Ian Stevenson, Twenty Cases Suggestive of Reincarnation (Charlottesville and London: University Of Virginia Press), ix-x)

Again:

> "I should regard disapprovingly anyone who, solely from reading this book, moved from skepticism—or ignorance—concerning reincarnation to a settled conviction that it occurs. I shall be content if I have succeeded in making the idea of reincarnation plausible to persons who have not thought it was; if some of them then think it worth their while to examine the evidence in my detailed case reports, I shall have accomplished more than I set out to do." (Ian Stevenson M.D., Children Who Remember Previous Lives: A Question of Reincarnation, rev. ed., 3 (Kindle Edition); Jefferson, North Carolina; McFarland & Company, Inc., Publishers)

Magic does not find its source from psychic energy.

Demonic Energy

The other source for magic is from demonic energy, i.e., power from the spirits of the deceased. Historically, this has been the understanding of the source of magic from many cultures around the world.

> "ONE OF THE CLEAREST WINDOWS FOR SEEING WHAT ORDINARY PEOPLE Believed about supernatural

74

powers in the New Testament era is the realm of magic and divination. Magical beliefs and practices were a part of all religious traditions (and even came to have a share in Christianity!). In Western culture we have come to think of magic as harmless trickery in the context of entertainment. When we speak of magic during the period of the New Testament, however, we must realize it was not the art of illusion. Magic represented a method of manipulating good and evil spirits to lend help or bring harm. Magical formulas could be used for such things as attracting a lover or winning a chariot race. Black magic, or sorcery, involved summoning spirits to accomplish all kinds of evil deeds. Curses could be placed, competitors subdued, and enemies restrained." (Clinton E. Arnold, Powers of Darkness: Principalities & Powers in Paul's Letters, 21 (Kindle Edition); Downers Grove, Illinois; InterVarsity Press)

The Eddas are filled with occult practices where magic is derived from the world of the dead. Simply consider the story of Mimir mentioned above. One Odinist writes:

"The head of Mimir seems to be the only example of a magical head in Norse lore, but severed heads are a staple of Celtic tradition and may have inspired the Scandinavian story. In Pagan Celtic Britain, Anne Ross devotes an entire chapter to the Cult of the Head. In Gaul, Celtic chieftains would preserve the heads of distinguished enemies in cedar oil and stone heads from ritual sites abound. In the Welsh Mabinogion, on their retreat from the war in Ireland, the gods carried with them the head of Bran the Blessed to advise and prophesy, and finally buried it beneath the Tower of London to guard Britain. The lore of early Ireland includes a number of stories in which placing a severed head in a well causes the well to become magical." (Diana L. Paxson, Odin: Ecstasy, Runes, & Norse Magic, 226-227 (Kindle Edition); Newburyport, MA; Weiser Books)

Indeed, this is very similar to occult practices that were taking place in the world before the Flood.

Ken Johnson notes:

"*Teraphim* The teraphim were idols used in ancestor worship. They were supposed to allow you to communicate with your ancestors at the proper astrological times. My guess is that the teraphim were not a new invention, but a continuation from the pre-flood world. There are two types of teraphim mentioned in the book of Jasher. The first type was created by taking the first born male of the family and cutting off his head. The victim's head was supposed to retain contact with the departed spirit. With the proper ritual, the mummified head could serve as a conduit to the spirit world, passing information between a family and their ancestor gods. The second type of teraphim was created by constructing an idol of the deceased and was used in the same way. The rituals had to be done at the proper astrological time. The ceremony used candles and other paraphernalia. Laban 's teraphim were the second type: little gold gods with the astrological tables carved on them, rather than the first type mentioned, the mummified head of a real ancestor. "And this is the manner of the images; in taking a man who is the first born and slaying him and taking the hair off his head, and taking salt and salting the head and anointing it in oil, then taking a small tablet of copper or a tablet of gold and writing the name upon it, and placing the tablet under his tongue, and taking the head with the tablet under the tongue and putting it in the house, and lighting up lights before it and bowing down to it. And at the time when they bow down to it, it speaketh to them in all matters that they ask of it, through the power of the name which is written in it. And some make them in the figures of men, of gold and silver, and go to them in times known to them, and the figures receive the influence of the stars, and tell them future things, and in this manner were the images which Rachel stole from her father, Laban." Jasher 31:41-43 In ancient Egypt, Canaan, and other places, archeologists have found communities with bones of infants buried in the walls of most homes. We can see this is connected to the teraphim form of ancestor worship. The ancient pagans believed that contacting the nature spirits helped in their evolution. The magic rites included blood rituals, burning candles, astrology, and idols/teraphim. The Egyptians had burial grounds for regular Egyptians (Jasher 14:13 14); but they buried their firstborn children in the walls of their homes. This was the Egyptian form of teraphim. Jasher records that when the death angel killed all the first born in Egypt, the angel also tore the remains of the sacrificed firstborn children out of the walls of the Egyptian houses (Jasher 80:44-46). This information indicates the plague of the firstborn was directed against the teraphim, showing that the God of Israel was superior to all the so called gods of Egypt, including all their ancestor gods!" (Ken Johnson, Ancient Paganism: The Sorcery Of The Fallen Angels, 54-56 (Kindle Edition))

Notice the similarities between the occult practices of the Canaanite, Egyptian, Celtic, and Norse religions regarding the use of teraphim for gaining occult knowledge from the spirit world.

In full harmony with this, the Bible is very clear that the magic powers of the pagans are fueled by demonic forces.

For example, the Bible tells us of the Egyptian sorcerers who confronted Moses:

Exodus 7:11—But Pharaoh also called the wise men and the sorcerers; so the magicians of Egypt, they also did in like manner with their enchantments.

Exodus 7:22—Then the magicians of Egypt did so with their enchantments; and Pharaoh's heart grew hard, and he did not heed them, as the LORD had said.

Exodus 8:7—And the magicians did so with their enchantments, and brought up frogs on the land of Egypt.

One of the ancient Jewish history books which the Bible references, the book of Jubilees, tells us the source of the sorcerers enchantments:

Jubilees 48:9-12. And the prince of the Mastêmâ stood up against thee, and sought to cast thee into the hands of

Pharaoh, and he helped the Egyptian sorcerers, and they stood up and wrought before thee. (10). The evils indeed we permitted them to work, but the remedies we did not allow to be wrought by their hands. (11). And the Lord smote them with malignant ulcers, and they were not able to stand for we destroyed them so that they could not perform a single sign. (12). And notwithstanding all (these) signs and wonders the prince of the Mastêmâ was not put to shame because he took courage and cried to the Egyptians to pursue after thee with all the powers of the Egyptians, with their chariots, and with their horses, and with all the hosts of the peoples of Egypt.

Other Scriptures make it clear that the spirits of the dead are able to produce seemingly miraculous events in the world of man.

Again:

2 Thessalonians 2:9—The coming of the lawless one is according to the working of Satan, with all power, signs, and lying wonders,

Revelation 16:14—For they are spirits of demons, performing signs, which go out to the kings of the earth and of the whole world, to gather them to the battle of that great day of God Almighty.

It is also worth noting that the power of the God of the Bible was always shown to be greater than the gods of the demons.

For example:

Exodus 7:12   For every man threw down his rod, and they became serpents. But Aaron's rod swallowed up their rods.

Exodus 8:18-19—Now the magicians so worked with their enchantments to bring forth lice, but they could not. So there were lice on man and beast. (19) Then the magicians said to Pharaoh, "This is the finger of God." But Pharaoh's heart grew hard, and he did not heed them, just as the LORD had said.

Exodus 9:11—And the magicians could not stand before Moses because of the boils, for the boils were on the magicians and on all the Egyptians.

Even the ancient Egyptians confirm these facts by reminding us that

"For example, one of the most well-known documents in Egyptology is the Ipuwer papyrus (officially known as Papyrus Leiden 344), which records an account remarkably similar to the plagues described in the book of Exodus. The papyrus was obtained by Swedish diplomat, Giovanni Anastasi, and sold to the Leiden Museum in Holland in 1828. No one realized the exact significance of the contents of the document until the first full translation was done in 1909 by a British Egyptologist, Alan H.Gardiner, under the title The Admonitions of an Egyptian Sage from a Hieratic Papyrus in Leiden. In addition, there have been many later full translations made, including an Oxford edition (2009). Currently, the document is stored at the National Museum of Antiquities in the Netherlands. Its contents are widely regarded by Egyptologists as a lamentation over the catastrophic conditions in Egypt written by a high Egyptian official named Ipuwer sometime prior to the thirteenth century BC (which is consistent with either an early or late chronology for the Exodus). Ipuwer was known as one of the great wise sages in Egyptian tian history. His astonishing description of the conditions, to the surprise of Egyptologists, appeared remarkably similar to the biblical account of the ten plagues recorded in the book of Exodus. The date of the Ipuwer manuscript approximately fits the Exodus date. The hieratic script style was in use at that time period, the events described are remarkably similar to the plagues, the location of the events (Egypt) matches the setting of the Exodus, and the odds of all these calamities occurring at the same time make them more than coincidental. There is no scientific, linguistic, or historical fact that Egyptologists can point to that would decisively preclude the content of the papyrus being a lament over the

Exodus plagues. A simple comparison of the content in both the book of Exodus and the Ipuwer papyrus leaves little doubt to their similarities (see table below)." (Joseph M. Holden & Norman Geisler, The Popular Handbook Of Archaeology And The Bible: Discoveries That Confirm The Reliability of Scripture, 2555-2568 (Kindle Edition); Eugene, Oregon; Harvest House Publishers).

Notice some ways that the Ipuwer Papyrus confirms the Bible account:

Exodus 4:9—And it shall be, if they do not believe even these two signs, or listen to your voice, that you shall take water from the river and pour it on the dry land. The water which you take from the river will become blood on the dry land."

Ipuwer 7:5—Behold, Egypt is fallen to the pouring of water. And he who poured water on the ground seizes the mighty in misery.

Exodus 7:20-21-20 And Moses and Aaron did so, just as the LORD commanded. So he lifted up the rod and struck the waters that were in the river, in the sight of Pharaoh and in the sight of his servants. And all the waters that were in the river were turned to blood. (21) The fish that were in the river died, the river stank, and the Egyptians could not drink the water of the river. So there was blood throughout all the land of Egypt.

Ipuwer 2:10—The River is blood. If you drink of it, you lose your humanity, and thirst for water.

Exodus 9:6, 23, 31—So the LORD did this thing on the next day, and all the livestock of Egypt died; but of the livestock of the children of Israel, not one died....And Moses stretched out his rod toward heaven; and the LORD sent thunder and hail, and fire darted to the ground. And the LORD rained hail on the land of Egypt....Now the flax and the barley were struck, for the barley was in the head and the flax was in bud.

Ipuwer 6:3; 3:3; 7:13—Gone is the barley of abundance.... Food supplies are running short. The nobles hunger and suffer.... . Those who had shelter are in the dark of the storm.

Exodus 10:15, 7—For they covered the face of the whole earth, so that the land was darkened; and they ate every herb of the land and all the fruit of the trees which the hail had left. So there remained nothing green on the trees or on the plants of the field throughout all the land of Egypt....Then Pharaoh's servants said to him, "How long shall this man be a snare to us? Let the men go, that they may serve the LORD their God. Do you not yet know that Egypt is destroyed?"

Ipuwer 3:13"What shall we do about it? All is ruin!

Exodus 12:29—And it came to pass at midnight that the LORD struck all the firstborn in the land of Egypt, from the firstborn of Pharaoh who sat on his throne to the firstborn of the captive who was in the dungeon, and all the firstborn of livestock.

Ipuwer 2:5, 6, 13; 4:3—Behold, plague sweeps the land, blood is everywhere, with no shortage of the dead.... He who buries his brother in the ground is everywhere.... Woe is me for the grief of this time.

Exodus 12:30—So Pharaoh rose in the night, he, all his servants, and all the Egyptians; and there was a great cry in Egypt, for there was not a house where there was not one dead.

Ipuwer 3:14—Wailing is throughout the land, mingled with lamentations.

Each one of the Ten Plagues demonstrated the power of God over an Egyptian god or goddess who claimed to be supreme in that particular category. For example, one Egyptian god, Khnum, claimed to reign over the Nike River. By Jehovah (the God of the Bible) turning the waters of the Nile to blood, He demonstrated He was greater than Khnum!

"Now I know that the LORD *is* greater than all the gods; for in the very thing in which they behaved proudly, *He was* above them."

Since magic is connected with demons, it is no surprise that the Bible condemns all forms of witchcraft:

> *1 Samuel 15:23—For rebellion is as the sin of witchcraft, And stubbornness is as iniquity and idolatry. Because you have rejected the word of the LORD, He also has rejected you from being king."*

What Norse Occultism Teaches Us about the Norse Religion

There are several lessons which may be drawn from teachings of the Eddas regarding the Norse religion.

First, Odin himself is clearly not God. He is a being who is lacking in knowledge, so much so that he seeks such from the world of the dead! He is a being who needs to sacrifice himself in order to pay for such occult knowledge. He resorts to human lusts, and is able to be injured and outwitted by his opponents.

Second, the Norse scriptures do not provide any evidence which demonstrate that they are inspired by God. They reflect gods who are deified humans at best. Contrast this with the Christian Scriptures, which have numerous evidences to demonstrate that they are inspired of God (in this series of lessons, we have seen evidences from prophecy and fulfillment and archaeology).

Third, the Norse religion and practice are based on occultism which is similar to that of surrounding nations and religions. The evidence we will consider next indicates a strong possibility that Odin is connected with the Nephilim of the Old Testament Scriptures.

Odin And The Nephilim

The Bible teaches us that there were a race of giant-like creatures (the Nephilim) who were born from the relations between fallen angels and human beings.

It is written:

> *Genesis 6:1-4—Now it came to pass, when men began to multiply on the face of the earth, and daughters were born to them, (2) that the sons of God saw the daughters of men, that they were beautiful; and they took wives for themselves of all whom they chose. (3) And the LORD said, "My Spirit shall not strive with man forever, for he is indeed flesh; yet his days shall be one hundred and twenty years." (4) There were giants on the earth in those days, and also afterward, when the sons of God came in to the daughters of men and they bore children to them. Those were the mighty men who were of old, men of renown.*

These nephilim (like the fallen angels who begat them) were extremely wicked and evil.

An ancient Jewish history book, the book of Enoch, tells us of them:

> 1 Enoch 7:1-6—"Each of the two hundred chose a wife for himself and they began to go in unto them and to mate with them, and they taught them sorcery and enchantments, and the cutting of roots, and made them acquainted with plants. (2) These women became pregnant and gave birth to great giants, whose height reached up to three thousand ells. (3) These giants consumed all the food; and when men could no longer sustain them, (4) the giants turned against them and devoured mankind. (5) They also began to sin against birds, and beasts, and reptiles, and fish, and to devour one another's flesh, and drink the blood. (6) Then the earth laid accusation against the lawless ones." (Ken Johnson, Ancient Book of Enoch, 18-19 (Kindle Edition))

It was this horrible transgression that led to God bringing the Great Flood (the Deluge) to cover the land and destroy from it all life (save for Noah and his family on the Ark with the animals).

However, it was also declared in Enoch that the spirits of the dead Nephilim which were killed in the Flood were left upon the Earth:

> 1 Enoch 15:8-12—My judgment for the giants is that since they are born from flesh they will be called evil spirits and will remain on the earth. (9) Because they were created from above, from the holy Watchers, at death their spirits will come forth from their bodies and dwell on the earth. They will be called evil spirits. (10) The heavenly spirits will dwell in heaven, but the terrestrial spirits who were born on earth will dwell on earth. (11)The evil spirits of the giants will be like clouds. They will afflict, corrupt, tempt, battle, work destruction on the earth, and do evil; they will not eat nor drink, but be invisible. (12) They will rise up against the children of men and against the women, because they have proceeded from them.

What is interesting in this regard with the Norse scriptures is that there are many connections between Odin and the giants!

> "'But evil men go to Hel and thence down to the Misty Hel; and that is down in the ninth world.' Then said Gangleri: 'What did he before heaven and earth were made?' And Harr answered: 'He was a then with the Rime0Giants?' (Prose Edda (Translated by Arthur Gilchrist Brodeur), 15 (Kindle Edition))

Indeed, there are over sixty references in the Prose Edda to the giants, and they are all in one way or another connected with Odin!

This contributes to the notion that Odin was (is) a demon.

The Magic Of Odin Like That Of The Nephilim

As noticed from the book of Jasher, the pre-flood world practiced a form of witchcraft with teraphim (the skulls of deceased humans which were used to channel the spirits of the

84

dead). We learned that this same type of sorcery is found in one of the most popular stories in Odinistic scripture.

Odin The Wanderer And The Nephilim

The Eddas are filled with examples of Odin being the traveling god, the Wanderer. He is not content to stay in Asgard, but instead declares his intention time and again to travel through the Nine Realms. Diana L. Paxson, in her book Odin; Ecstasy, Runes, & Norse Magic (24-26, Kindle Edition; Newburyport, MA; Weiser Books) provides some fantastic examples.

- Odin gets into an argument with Thor in Harbardsljodh (in the Eddas) and says that he had been traveling in distant lands and seducing various women.

- Odin goes to the underworld (Hel) in order to consult with Volva, according to Baldrsdraumr.

- Odin claims to be Vegtam (the Way Tamer) and also the son of Valtan ("Tamer of the Slain").

Many other examples are cited.

What is of special interest is how Jesus describes demons as being wandering spirits:

> *Matthew 12:43-45—When an unclean spirit goes out of a man, he goes through dry places, seeking rest, and finds none. (44) Then he says, 'I will return to my house from which I came.' And when he comes, he finds it empty, swept, and put in order. (45) Then he goes and takes with him seven other spirits more wicked than himself, and they enter and dwell there; and the last state of that man is worse than the first. So shall it also be with this wicked generation."*

> *Luke 11:24-26- "When an unclean spirit goes out of a man, he goes through dry places, seeking rest; and finding none, he says, 'I will return to my house from which I came.' (25) And when he comes, he finds it swept and put in order. (26) Then he goes and takes with him seven other spirits more*

wicked than himself, and they enter and dwell there; and the last state of that man is worse than the first. "

The Lord describes the demons as wandering through "dry places." The phrase "dry places" had reference to what was written by the Prophet Isaiah some seven hundred years before Jesus Christ was born into the world:

Isaiah 13:20-22—It will never be inhabited, Nor will it be settled from generation to generation; Nor will the Arabian pitch tents there, Nor will the shepherds make their sheepfolds there. (21) But wild beasts of the desert will lie there, And their houses will be full of owls; Ostriches will dwell there, And wild goats will caper there. (22) The hyenas will howl in their citadels, And jackals in their pleasant palaces. Her time is near to come, And her days will not be prolonged. "

Isaiah 34:14—The wild beasts of the desert shall also meet with the jackals, And the wild goat shall bleat to its companion; Also the night creature shall rest there, And find for herself a place of rest.

Isaiah 34:14 (CEV)-Wildcats and hyenas will hunt together, demons will scream to demons, and creatures of the night will live among the ruins.

The ancient Hebrews saw a connection between animals and the spirit world. While everything God created was good (Genesis 1:31), our Earth is in a fallen state because of sin (Genesis 3:17-19; Romans 8:19-22). The Jewish people recognized that demons may take the form of animals (cf. Genesis 3:1-6), and that there are aspects of creatures in the fallen world which powerfully portray the nature of wicked spirits.

Indeed, to notice that more than animals are meant in this passage, we need to only look at the Book of Revelation, where John references this passage to describe the "Babylon" of his day and age (i.e., Rome):

Revelation 18:2—And he cried mightily with a loud voice, saying, "Babylon the great is fallen, is fallen, and has become a dwelling place of demons, a prison for every foul spirit, and a cage for every unclean and hated bird!

Notice the clear reference here to Isaiah 13 and 34, and the connection between "demons," "foul spirits," and "unclean and hated birds" (i.e., the animal kingdom).

Look closely at the phrases used in Isaiah 13 and 34:

"2. "Howling Creature" ('iyyîm); "Wild Beasts" (ṣiyyîm); "Lilith" (lîlît) The terminology of this section will no doubt be unfamiliar and strange. But to a culture that held the desert wilderness to be a place of frightful beings associated with the underworld, "the desert [was] populated by phantom-like creatures." Frey-Anthes summarizes the association of wild, deserted places with perceived dark powers: The concept of a subdivided world which is present in the Old Testament texts leads to the idea of animals and not clearly definable creatures, who are the inhabitants of a counterworld to human civilisation. Included among the eerie and dangerous animals who haunt deserted places.…

"The following are mostly called "desert-demons": Those who live in the ruins …

"As the name of the [ṣiyyîm] explains where they dwell ("those who belong to the dry landscape/desert dwellers"), the expression ['iyyîm] has rather got an onomatopoeic nature, it defines a howling creature ("howler").…

"The pair ['iyyîm] and [ṣiyyîm] belongs to the description of a destroyed city in Isa 13:21f.; Isa 34:14 and Jer 50:39.…

"The texts, however, speak of ghosts living at the periphery but they avoid a clear identification, which would be needed for an incantation, to identify the evil forces it wants to drive away. The creatures are described ambiguously in order to underline the vagueness of the peripheral counterworld. Two of the passages noted above deserve some attention. In Isaiah 13:21–22, a description of the impending devastation of Babylon, the terms ṣiyyîm and 'iyyîm occur in tandem with the śĕʿîrîm (Isa 13:21) associated with illegitimate sacrifices in Leviticus 17:7 (cf. Deut 32:12). The same grouping is present in Isaiah 34:14, a passage that adds lîlît to the assemblage—the Hebrew spelling of the well-known Mesopotamian demon-goddess Lilith: The "wind-demoness" Lilith, who can already be found in the Sumerian Epos "Gilgames, Enkidu and the Underworld" does not seem to have had any special importance outside Mesopotamia. Interpretations of supposed findings from Ugarit and Phoenicia are very uncertain. It is astonishing, however, that, according to Isa 34:14, Lilith belongs to the inhabitants of the counter world together with owls and other birds of prey, ostrich, jackals, snakes, desert dwellers, howlers and he-goats. The description of the ruins of Edom in Isa 34:11–15 is a subtly composed literary text with close connections to Isa 13:21f. and Jer 50:39, which are similar descriptions of the deserted Babylon. Isa 34:11–15 intensifies the descriptions of Isa 13:21f. and Jer 50:39 by listing the inhabitants of the periphery in a detailed way and by introducing Lilith. As Janowski notes, these terms could very naturally speak of "zoologically definable animals, i.e. nocturnal consumers of carrion, who appear in pairs or in packs," but "their association with theriomorphic demons ... and the demon Lilith, is intended to place the aspect of the counterhuman world in the foreground." . (Michael S. Heiser, Demons: What the Bible Really Says About the Powers of Darkness, 629-662 (Kindle Edition); Bellingham, Wa; Lexham Press)

Demons inhabit desolate areas. "Desolate" means empty, broken, uninhabited. Luke's account adds that they seek to find "rest.' Some believe that this means that they seek to find flesh to dwell in (since they once resided in the flesh). Could it be that the demons wish to "re-live" the experiences of the flesh which they had once enjoyed?

Observe that Jesus characterizes demons as beings which "wander" in the world of man.

Odin certainly falls into this category of being a wandering spirit who travels through dry places.

The Afterlife

Odinists teaching regarding the Afterlife affirms that most people will simply be reincarnated in their family lunge until they eventually welcomed by Odin into Valhalla. As we have seen, this is not true.

Jesus Christ provided the ultimate Payment for our moral sin and transgression. He died for us (in our place), was buried, and arose from the dead on the third day. This event-the resurrection of Jesus Christ-has been attested by over five hundred witnesses!

> *1 Corinthians 15:1-8—Moreover, brethren, I declare to you the gospel which I preached to you, which also you received and in which you stand, (2) by which also you are saved, if you hold fast that word which I preached to you—unless you believed in vain. (3) For I delivered to you first of all that which I also received: that Christ died for our sins according to the Scriptures, (4) and that He was buried, and that He rose again the third day according to the Scriptures, (5) and that He was seen by Cephas, then by the twelve. (6) After that He was seen by over five hundred brethren at once, of whom the greater part remain to the present, but some have fallen asleep. (7) After that He was seen by James, then by all the apostles. (8) Then last of all He was seen by me also, as by one born out of due time.*

God graciously offers salvation to whoever will come to Him through Jesus Christ:

> *Luke 9:23-26—Then He said to them all, "If anyone desires to come after Me, let him deny himself, and take up his cross daily, and follow Me. (24) For whoever desires to save his life will lose it, but whoever loses his life for My sake will save it. (25) For what profit is it to a man if he gains the whole world, and is himself destroyed or lost? (26) For whoever is ashamed of Me and My words, of him the Son of*

Man will be ashamed when He comes in His own glory, and in His Father's, and of the holy angels.

Mark 16:15-16—And He said to them, "Go into all the world and preach the gospel to every creature. (16) He who believes and is baptized will be saved; but he who does not believe will be condemned.

Acts 2:38—Then Peter said to them, "Repent, and let every one of you be baptized in the name of Jesus Christ for the remission of sins; and you shall receive the gift of the Holy Spirit.

Acts 22:16—And now why are you waiting? Arise and be baptized, and wash away your sins, calling on the name of the Lord.'

For baptized believers who turn away from the Lord in sin, Jesus calls them back to forgiveness and restoration

1 John 1:9—If we confess our sins, He is faithful and just to forgive us our sins and to cleanse us from all unrighteousness.

Revelation 3:20—Behold, I stand at the door and knock. If anyone hears My voice and opens the door, I will come in to him and dine with him, and he with Me.

The churches of Christ stand ready to assist you.
The grace of the Lord Jesus Christ, and the love of God, and the communion of the Holy Spirit, be with you all. Amen.

Questions

1. What is a teraphim?

   _____

2. What three stories from the Eddas regarding Odin are some of the most well-known?

   _____

   _____

   _____

3. Who was Mimir?

   _____

4. What are two evidences that we have studied in these lessons which show that the Bible is the Word of God?

   _____

   _____

5. What were the Nephilim?

   _____

   _____

6. What did Ian Stevenson state regarding the evidences for the theory of reincarnation?

   _____

   _____

   _____

7. 1 Enoch 15:8-12-My judgment for the _____ is that since they are born from flesh they will be called _____ _____ and will remain on the _____. 9 Because they were created from above, from the holy _____, at death their spirits will come forth from their bodies and dwell on the earth. They will be called evil spirits. 10 The heavenly spirits will dwell in heaven, but the _____ spirits who were born on earth will dwell on earth. 11 The evil spirits of the giants will be like _____. They will

   _____, _____, _____, _____, work _____ on the earth, and do _____; they will not eat nor drink, but be _____. 12 They will rise up against the children of men and against the women, because they have _____ from them.

8. What does the word "rune" mean?

   _____

   _____

9. What is the Doctrine Of Emanations?

_____

_____

10. Who is Khnum?

_____

11. What are some problems with pantheism?

_____

_____

_____

12. Acts 2:28-Then Peter said to them, "_____, and let every one of you be _____ in the name of _____ _____ for the _____ of sins; and you shall receive the _____ of the Holy Spirit.

13. What are two proposed sources of magic?

_____

14. What are some Bible passages which describe demons as spirits which wander?

_____

_____

_____

15. List some examples of how the Ipuwer Papyrus documents the events of the Exodus?
Exodus 18:11—Now I know that the LORD *is* _____ than all the _____; for in the very thing in which they behaved _____, *He was* above them."

16. Mark 16:16-He who _____ and is _____ will be _____; but he who does not believe will be condemned.

Lesson Four

Buddhism

Origins

The religion known as Buddhism had its' beginning in the country of India, with a man named Siddhartha Gautama. It was said that he was the tenth and last reincarnation of the Buddha (the "enlightened one"). Steve Cioccolanti, a former Buddhist, provides great historical information about the man who became known as the Buddha:

"Buddha was born on April 8 in Lumpini Park, a garden in ancient India or present day Nepal. Seven days later his mother Queen Maya died. He was subsequently raised by his mother's younger sister Maha-prajapati. Five days after birth his father King Suddhodana received a prophecy from 8 brahmins that Siddhartha had the potential to become a great man. Asita said, "If he does not become a great holy man, he will become a great king. If he becomes a holy man, he will become the greatest founder of the greatest religion in the world." But the youngest of the brahmins named Gaundinya spoke up and said, "No, he must become a monk and he will become enlightened and the founder of a great religion." His father, being a king, understandably did not like the idea of his son becoming a monk, so he decided to shield his son from religious teachings and the knowledge of human suffering. He tried to make him enjoy comfort and only see the pleasures of life. In fact, he built 3 palaces for his young son so he could be comfortable during each of the 3 seasons of the year. At the age of 16 he married a young princess, a cousin named Yasotara. They were married for 13 years. At the age of 29, he had his first and only son named Rahula or Rahun in Thai. It was around this time that the Prince left his palace and saw four different people: an elderly person, a sick person, a dead person and lastly a priest. He saw that after humans are born, they suffer from old age, illness, and death. The thought came to him that everybody suffers and no one could escape the suffering. This was the problem that troubled his heart, he thought about this over and over. He wanted a way out of this vicious cycle–the "wheel of suffering". Then he thought that in life there is duality. If there's hot, there's cold. If there's suffering (birth, aging, sickness, death), then there must be something opposite (no birth, no suffering, no pain, no death). The prince saw the happiness of the world as an illusion and the true purpose of life is to escape the cycle of suffering. The only way to escape the cycle of suffering is to be liberated from the cycle of life. He considered that one way to achieve this was to become celibate and a monk. So at the age of 29 he abandoned his newborn baby Rahula and his wife Yasotara. At first he made a decision to become a sadhu, or a monk within the Hindu religion. He cut his hair, changed his clothes, and changed his status from being a very rich person to becoming a very poor person. Whatever he had remaining he gave to his servant Channa to take home. He tried to follow two Hindu brahman teachers but felt Hinduism did not provide the answer. He left to find his own way. Soon he had five disciples following him. After 6 years of living as an ascetic in the forest, punishing his body, fasting, praying, and meditating, he gave up. He went bathing in a river and accepted a bowl of milk pudding from a woman named Sujata. At this his five disciples were very shocked. Sorely disappointed, they left him. Alone, Siddhartha continued his search for a way out of the cycle of suffering, choosing a more moderate path. Legend has it that he sat under a fig tree and vowed not to get up until he was enlightened. At the age of 35, he became enlightened. This historically meant the divide of Hinduism and Buddhism. Buddha actually split from the Hindu tradition and the teachings of the brahmans and started a new religion." (Steve Cioccolanti, FROM BUDDHA TO JESUS: An Insider's View of Buddhism & Christianity

94

(Comparative World Religions), 17-19 (Kindle Edition); Discover Media)

God

Buddhism is not overtly atheistic, despite the teaching of some. Instead, Buddhists hold to a doctrine similar to panentheism. This belief system is the notion that God inhabits the universe as a spirit inhabits a body. It is claimed that thereby God is in a constant state of change.

Karma And Samsara

Buddhists teach that each person must pay off his karmic debt, and this is done by a continuous cycle of reincarnation (being born again into a new body after a person dies physically). This cycle of reincarnation is known as Samsara.

Let's look closer at karma.

"The literal meaning of karma (as we encountered it in karma yoga) is work, but as a doctrine it means, roughly, the moral law of cause and effect. Science has alerted the West to the importance of causal relationships in the physical world. Every physical event, we are inclined to believe, has its cause, and every cause will have its determinate effects. India extends this concept of causation to include moral and spiritual life as well. To some extent the West has as well. "As a man sows, so shall he reap"; or again, "Sow a thought and reap an act, sow an act and reap a habit, sow a habit and reap a character; sow a character and reap a destiny"—these are ways the West has put the point. The difference is that India tightens up and extends its concept of moral law to see it as absolute; it brooks no exceptions. The present condition of each interior life—how happy it is, how confused or serene, how much it sees—is an exact product of what it has wanted and done in the past. Equally, its present thoughts and decisions are determining its future experiences. Each act that is directed upon the world has its equal and opposite

95

reaction on oneself. Each thought and deed delivers an unseen chisel blow that sculpts one's destiny. This idea of karma and the completely moral universe it implies carries two important psychological corollaries. First, it commits the Hindu who understands it to complete personal responsibility. Each individual is wholly responsible for his or her present condition and will have exactly the future he or she is now creating. Most people are not willing to admit this. They prefer, as the psychologists say, to project—to locate the source of their difficulties outside themselves. They want excuses, someone to blame so that they may be exonerated. This, say the Hindus, is immature. Everybody gets exactly what is deserved—we have made our beds and must lie in them. Conversely, the idea of a moral universe closes the door on chance or accident. Most people have little idea how much they secretly bank on luck—hard luck to justify past failures, good luck to bring future successes. How many people drift through life simply waiting for the breaks, for that moment when a lucky lottery number brings riches and a dizzying spell of fame. If you approach life this way, says Hinduism, you misjudge your position pathetically. Breaks have nothing to do with protracted levels of happiness, nor do they happen by chance. We live in a world in which there is no chance or accident. Those words are simply covers for ignorance. Because karma implies a lawful world, it has often been interpreted as fatalism. However often Hindus may have succumbed to this interpretation, it is untrue to the doctrine itself. Karma decrees that every decision must have its determinate consequences, but the decisions themselves are, in the last analysis, freely arrived at. To approach the matter from the other direction, the consequences of one's past decisions condition one's present lot, as a card player finds himself dealt a particular hand while remaining free to play that hand in a variety of ways. This means that the career of a soul as it threads its course through innumerable human bodies is guided by its choices, which are controlled by what the soul wants and wills at each stage of the journey. What its wants are, and the order in which they appear, can be summarized quickly here, for previous sections have considered them at length. When it first enters a human body, a jiva (soul) wants nothing more than to taste widely of the sense delights its new physical equipment makes possible. With repetition, however, even the most ecstatic of these falls prey to habituation and grows monotonous, whereupon the jiva turns to social conquests to escape boredom. These conquests—the various modes of wealth, fame, and power—can hold the individual's interest for a considerable time. The stakes are high and their attainment richly gratifying. Eventually, however, this entire program of personal ambition is seen for what it is: a game—a fabulous, exciting, history-making game, but a game all the same. As long as it holds one's interest, it satisfies. But when novelty wears off, when a winner has acknowledged with the same bow and pretty little speech the accolades that have come so many times before, he or she begins to yearn for something new and more deeply satisfying. Duty, the total dedication of one's life to one's community, can fill the need for a while, but the ironies and anomalies of history make this object too a revolving door. Lean on it and it gives, but in time one discovers that it is going round and round. After social dedication the only good that can satisfy is one that is infinite and eternal, whose realization can turn all experience, even the experience of time and apparent defeat, into splendor, as storm clouds drifting through a valley look different viewed from a peak that is bathed in sunshine. The bubble is approaching the water's surface and is demanding final release. The soul's progress through these ascending strata of human wants does not take the form of a straight line with an acute upward angle. It fumbles and zigzags its way toward what it really needs. In the long run, however, the trend of attachments will be upward—everyone finally gets the point. By "upward" here is meant a gradual relaxation of attachment to physical objects and stimuli, accompanied by a progressive release from self-interest. We can almost visualize the action of karma as it delivers the consequences of what the soul reaches out for. It is as if each desire that aims at the ego's gratification adds a grain of concrete to the wall that surrounds the individual self and insulates it from the infinite sea of being that surrounds it; while, conversely, each compassionate or disinterested act dislodges a grain from the confining dike. Detachment cannot be overtly assessed, however; it has no public index. The fact that someone withdraws to a monastery is no proof of triumph over self and craving, for these may continue to abound in the imaginations of the heart. Conversely, an executive may be heavily involved in worldly responsibilities; but if he or she manages them detachedly—living in the world as a mudfish lives in the mud, without the mud's sticking to it— the world becomes a ladder to ascend. Never during its pilgrimage is the human spirit completely adrift and alone. From start to finish its nucleus is the Atman, the God within, exerting pressure to "out" like a jack-in-the-box. Underlying its whirlpool of transient feelings, emotions, and delusions is the self-luminous, abiding point of the transpersonal God. Though it is buried too deep in the soul to be normally noticed, it is the sole ground of human existence and awareness. As the sun lights the world even when cloud-covered, "the Immutable is never seen but is the Witness; It is never heard but is the Hearer; it is never thought, but is the Thinker; is never known, but is the Knower. There is no other witness but This, no other knower but This." 32 But God is not only the empowering agent in the soul's every action. In the end it is God's radiating warmth that melts the soul's icecap, turning it into a pure capacity for God. What happens then? Some say the individual soul passes into complete identification with God and loses every trace of its former separateness. Others, wishing to taste sugar, not be sugar, cherish the hope that some slight differentiation between the soul and God will still remain—a thin line upon the ocean that provides nevertheless a remnant of personal identity that some consider indispensable for the beatific vision." (Huston

Smith, The World's Religions, 68-71 (Kindle Edition); New York, NY; HarperCollins Publishers, Inc.)

In Buddhism, any suffering which a person suffers in this life is a direct result of something which he did in a past life which has brought on this condition.

Nirvana

According to Buddhism, each person is born paying for the karma of his past life. We are told that each person must pay for all of his past evil deeds and be rewarded for his past good deeds as he is reincarnated into the world. Supposedly, over several lifetimes, a person is able to achieve the goal of ending all desire by practicing the Eightfold Path. He thus is able to pay for his karmic debt, which in turn leads to his eventually entering into a spiritual state of known as Nirvana, where all individuality and desire are cancelled out.

Nirvana is very difficult to describe, seeing as how even Buddha himself did not define it.

"In its shortest form Buddha's teaching may be summarized as follows: Birth is sorrow, age is sorrow, sickness is sorrow, death is sorrow, clinging to earthly things is sorrow. Birth and rebirth, the chain of reincarnation, result from the thirst for life together with passion and desire. The only escape from this thirst is to follow the Eightfold Path: Right belief, right resolve, right word, right act, right life, right effort, right thinking, right meditation. The goal of Buddhism is Nirvana. A definition of this term is almost impossible for the simple reason that Buddha himself gave no clear idea, and in all probability possessed none, of this state. He was indeed asked by more than 4. Nirvana, one of his disciples whether Nirvana was postmundane or postcelestial existence, or whether it was annihilation. To all these questions, however, he refused an answer, for it was characteristic of his teachings that they were practically confined to the present life, and concerned themselves but little either with problems of merely academic philosophy or with the unknowable. Some measure of light, however, may be gained from the orthodox systems of Indian philosophy which are based upon the doctrine of the divine inspiration of the Veda. According to all of these, the aummum bonum is release from karma and reincarnation, a goal which is to be attained by knowledge, and which consists in absorption into or reimion with the Over-Soul. This involves the annihilation of individuality, and in this sense Nirvana is nihilism, so that with the tacit ignoring of any real conception of the divine in the teachings of Buddha, Nirvana seems to imply the annihilation of the soul rather than its absorption. It is noteworthy, furthermore, that the word Nirvana etymologically denotes " a blowing out." the extinguishing of the fires of hatred, infatuation, and all passions. Nirvana seems to have been twofold, a secondary condition which may be reached by the righteous in this life, and the blessed state of freedom from rebirth." (Johann Jakob Herzog & Philip Schaffer, The new Schaff-Herzog Encyclopedia Of Religious Knowledge, Embracing Biblical, Historical, Doctrinal, And Practical Theology And Biblical, Theological, And Ecclesiastical Biography (Volume Two), 17869-17888 (Kindle Edition); Funk & Wagnalls Company)

Holy Scriptures Of Buddhism

There are several books of scripture in Buddhism, but the most reliable text is the Pali Tripitaka. Most of the other Buddhist sects start with these books, and then add to them.

"In Theravada Buddhism there are three groups of writings considered to be holy scriptures, known as "The Three Baskets" (Tripitaka). The Vinaya Pitaka (discipline basket) contains rules for the higher class of Buddhists; the Sutta Pitaka (teaching basket) contains the discourses of the Buddha; and the Abidhamma Pitaka (metaphysical basket) contains Buddhist theology. The total volume of these three groups of writings is about 11 times larger than the Bible. In Mahayana Buddhism the scriptures are much more voluminous, as Clark B. Offner reveals: "A Mahayanist is one who reads Mahayana scriptures" is the definition given by one ancient Buddhist scholar. In contrast to the comparatively limited scope of the Pali canon used by Theravada Buddhists, Mahayana scriptures have multiplied to the point where standard editions of the Chinese canon encompass over 5,000 volumes. While the oldest scriptures are based on Sanskrit and contain much that is parallel to the Pali canon, other scriptures which have no Sanskrit prototypes have been written in Nepalese, Tibetan and Chinese. Since there are no clear limits to the Mahayana "canon," comparatively recent works by later innovators are often given de facto canonical status in the sects which adhere to their teachings. As there are such a number and such a variety of scriptures, most Mahayana sects have chosen certain favorite ones to which they refer exclusively. The fact is that some such selection is necessary, for this extreme bulk and breadth of the scriptures makes it impossible for believers to be acquainted with, let alone understand and practice, the often contradictory teachings found in them." (Josh McDowell & Bill Wilson, A Ready Defense: The Best Of Josh McDowell, 279-280 (Kindle Edition); Nashville, TN; Thomas Nelson, Inc.)

The Four Noble Truths

Buddhism's primary creed is that of the Four Noble Truths.

1. All Life Is Suffering.
2. All Suffering Is Due To Desire.
3. Suffering Ceases When Desire Ceases.
4. Freedom From Suffering Is Possible by Following The Eightfold Path.

What is the Eightfold Path?

1. Right View.
2. Right Intention.

3. Right Speech.

4. Right Action.

5. Right Livelihood.

6. Right Effort.

7. Right Mindfulness.

8. Right Concentration.

In Buddhism, the Eightfold Path is also known as "The Middle Path."

Logical Problems With The Basic Teachings Of Buddhism
Logical Problems With The Panentheistic Concept Of God

The Buddhist teaching of God is basically panentheistic, which is the belief that the universe is the body of God. In this belief system, everything in existence is an extension of God. This view of God is akin to the Cabalistic teaching known as the Doctrine Of Emanations.

Ken Johnson writes:

"One might understand if Lucifer was angry with God, he might convince one third of the angels of heaven to leave heaven to be alone, away from God. But look at the verses given about Lucifer's fall. He wanted to be worshiped as God and actually tried to take God's throne. How could any rational being think for one second that he might have power enough to force the only creator God out of His throne? No rational being would. Nor would Lucifer; unless, he believed his own lie. What was Lucifer's lie? Lucifer's lie was this: God is not separate from His creation. When God puts His spirit into a newly created being, He loses part of Himself. In the Jewish Kabala this concept is called the Doctrine of Emanations. In other words, if God created 100 billion people and put His spirit into each one of them, at that point the Bible would say God is still 100% God and

Man is 0% God. Lucifer, on the other hand, would say at that point God might be, say, 47% God and all humans collectively would equate to 53% God. Lucifer might have actually believed that if there were enough angels they could overcome God and absorb the rest of what God once was. That, in effect, would kill off God. He probably believed this was the way it had been done for generations of gods /angels and universes. The Doctrine of Emanations would become the basis of all future pagan religions on earth, and the primary cause of the earth's destruction by a world wide flood." (Ken Johnson, Th.D. *Ancient Paganism: The Sorcery Of The Fallen Angels,* 19 (Kindle Edition))

Here are some of the problems with panentheism.

First, God must be eternal (see our Evidence Of God's Existence—Part One) and yet we know that the universe had a beginning.

"Robert Jastrow, founder and former director of NASA's Goddard Institute for Space Studies, has summarized marized the evidence in his book God and the Astronomers, saying, "Now three lines of evidence-the motions of the galaxies, the laws of thermodynamics, and the life story of the stars-pointed to one conclusion: all indicated that the Universe had a beginning." (Norman Geisler & Ronald Brooks, When Skeptics Ask: A Handbook On Christian Evidences, 220 (Kindle Edition); Grand Rapids, Michigan; Baker Books)

The fact that the universe had a beginning shows us that panentheism cannot be true.

Second, pantheism asserts that God is always in a state of change. However, if that is the case, then change could never really be understood or recognized. In order for change to exist, there must be an unchanging standard by which the change is determined and observed. The fact that we can recognize change at all is proof that the perfect unchanging Standard exists (i.e., God).

This can be illustrated by contemplating the nature of truth and error.

> "Error does not prove skepticism, it refutes it. Josiah Royce's essay "The Possibility of Error" (in The Religious Aspect of Philosophy) proved that the possibility of error is necessarily grounded in, and logically presupposes, poses, the knowability of objective truth. To simplify the argument: We do indeed err, as the skeptic says. But we are also sometimes aware of our error; we can judge our errors as errors and correct them. The only way we could ever do this is by using a standard to measure the error as erroneous, as failing to come up to the standard. That standard cannot also be in error, otherwise we could never know that the original error is in error; for it is only by the authority of the standard that we can judge the original error to be an error. Thus the very concept of "error" presupposes some certain knowledge of truth." (Peter Kreeft & Ronald K. Tacelli, Handbook of Christian Apologetics: Hundreds of Answers to Crucial Questions, 368-369 (Kindle Edition); Downers Grove, Illinois; InterVarsity Press)

Third, morality poses a serious issue with panentheism. Every culture throughout time has recognized that certain principles are absolute, transcending culture and even religion. Geisler has well written:

> "Moral absolutes are unavoidable. Total moral relativism reduces to statements such as "You should never say never," "You should always avoid using always," or "You absolutely ought not believe in moral absolutes." "Ought" statements are moral statements, and "ought never" statements are absolute moral statements. So, there is no way to avoid moral absolutes without affirming a moral absolute. Total moral relativism is self-defeating." (Norman L. Geisler, Baker Encyclopedia of Christian Apologetics (Baker Reference Library), 501 (Kindle Edition); Grand Rapids, Michigan; Baker Books)

Yet if panentheism were true, then there could be no such standard of morality. Since God would constantly be changing (according to panentheism), then objective morality could not exist.

The fact of objective morality demonstrates another serious problem with panentheism.

Of course, the biggest problem with panentheism is that panentheists teach that both God and the universe are in a constant state of change. However, if there is no unchanging standard of change by which change is being measured, then how could change ever be known or catalogued?

> "Also, how can one know that everything is changing if there is not some unchanging standard by which to measure change? Because we are moving along with it, we don't notice that the world is rotating on its axis or revolving around the sun. It feels like we are standing still. The same thing happens if we toss a ball straight up in the air in an airplane. We don't realize that the ball is really traveling at 500 miles per hour because we are moving at the same speed. We can only be sure that something is moving when we measure it by something that is not moving. So how can we know that everything is changing unless we can look at something that is not changing? Panentheism has no explanation for this because it holds that even God is constantly changing." (Norman L. Geisler & Ronald M. Brooks, When Skeptics Ask: A Handbook On Christian Evidences, 47-51 (Kindle Edition); Grand Rapids, Michigan; Baker Books)

The very fact that change is taking place is evidence that there is an unchanging standard which precedes and supersedes both the change and the object undergoing change. This is unchanging Source is God Himself.

Malachi 3:6—For I am the LORD, I do not change; Therefore you are not consumed, O sons of Jacob.

The Four Noble Truths are a great example of self-contradiction.

It is claimed that the purpose of existence is to stamp out all desire: yet in order to stamp out all desire you must first cultivate the desire to do so! How can you stamp out all desire without first having the desire to do so? Yet if you stamp out all desire, then this includes the desire to stamp out all desire, which is contradictory.

Mike Robinson has well written:

> "The First NT is that life is basically suffering (dukkha). This means that the soul is out of harmony and seeks after the wrong things, and thus perpetuates the suffering. The Second NT is a result of desire. All men suffer because we lack that which we want and receive the trouble, which we do not desire. This desire to have and to possess things is the cause of our suffering. An important part of enlightenment is the understanding that suffering is just an illusion, like desire, and one escapes this desire through following the Dharma (the law of life, one's duty within cultural norms or the basic philosophical principals of one's life in the world). Van Til observed that "when apples are shaken off a tree, one can ask whether there must not have been some sort of something that is higher than the apples in order to account for the fruit. Similarly, not looking for the meaning of man in the light of the revelation that comes from Christ revealed in the Bible is even more absurd. He who does not look for the meaning of humanity in the light of the revelation that comes from God revealed in Scripture is like one who shakes off all the apples of the apple tree, grubs out the tree, and then asks whether there must not have been some sort of something that is higher than the apples in order to account for them. This 'some sort of something' or at most some sort of tree may, possibly or probably, tell us that it is an apple tree."

"More Noble Truths The Third NT is to strive to remove desire, and affirm that everything that seems real—things we seek—are all just illusions.

"• If all desire is error and increases suffering,

"• Then the desire to rid myself of desire is an error and actually increases suffering.

"• I should not desire to completely stifle desire.

"• I should desire Christ.

"One must control one's own mind. … and Remove all the impurities of worldly passion and egoism. The Fourth NT instructs one how to extinguish desire which, as asserted above, is self-impaling. On this crucial issue—the diagnosis of the human problem—Christianity and Buddhism are infinitely different. Buddha teaches that our desires need to be subdued and annihilated, but Jesus presses men to cultivate passionate desires to please God and follow after love. Buddha attempts to rid men of suffering by denying one's aspirations and in promulgating the notion that desires are part of the vast illusion of life. This reveals that the real need that Buddhists have is for the forgiveness of sins and acceptance by God. Only Jesus can provide this solution. The Buddhist is taught to resolve to follow Dharma with precision so one can find Nirvana. By contrast, the Christian, by grace, obtains salvation as a gift from God through the person and work of Christ.

"• All men sin.

"• Buddhism fails to offer an atonement for sin.

"• Christianity supplies an eternal atonement through Christ.

"• One should reject Buddha and accept Christ.

As is the case with all non-Christian religions, Buddhism lacks the epistemic environment to supply the a priori conditions for reason. It teaches an anti-reason paradigm, and beyond that, is essentially illogical. According to

Buddhism, all human experience is a mere illusion; and the world is rightly comprehended by antirational understanding because the world and all human experience are not real. This illusion must be affirmed to gain enlightenment. One must reject logic, truth, and reality to advance towards Nirvana.

"• One must employ reason to promote the Buddhist teaching of anti-reason.

"• Anti-reason is self-contradictory.

"• Buddhism rejects the laws of reason; thus, it is self-contradictory, as it employs reason to reject reason.

"• That which is self-contradictory is false.

"• Buddhism is false." (Mike Robinson, Christian Philosophy and Presuppositional Apologetics Examine Buddhism: Refuting The Religion of Buddha at Its Foundation (Presuppositional Apologetics and World Religions Book 7), 12-15 (Kindle Edition); Granbury, TX; Applied Apologetics Press, Inc.)

In the same ways, the Eight-Fold Path is untenable and illogical.

In contrast to this, Christianity is based upon words of truth and reason.

Acts 26:25—But he said, "I am not mad, most noble Festus, but speak the words of truth and reason.

Logical Problems With Karma

It is claimed by Buddha that the purpose of existence is to rid ourselves of the karmic debt of our past lives. Supposedly, by doing enough good deeds, we will be able to somehow cancel our penalty for the misdeeds of our past lives. Nevertheless, this presents several logical problems.

First, to whom are we indebted to pay for our sins? Buddhism makes no direct claims regarding the existence and nature of God, yet the very fact of moral law demands the existence of the Moral Lawgiver (i.e., God).

Second, what makes Buddhists think it is possible to pay for the debt of our misdeeds? Can we ever truly know the full impact of a single wrong deed? Who besides God Himself is able to fully understand the far-reaching results of even a single sin? As a pebble thrown in a pond creates ripples that may go further then we can so, so iniquity does more harm than we can be known and realized.

What makes Buddhists think that enough good deeds could ever 'balance out' the sinful deeds of even one lifetime?

Third, assuming for the sake of argument that reincarnation is true, even if embracing the Four Noble Truths by means of the Eightfold Path could pay for the karmic debt of a past life, what about the karmic debt achieved in this present life? Buddhism can never actually provide hope of forgiveness and redemption, but would instead lead to an infinite regress, which would lead to an infinite number of contradictions, again showing Buddhism to be self-contradictory and illogical.

> "Actual infinites are sets of numbers to which no increment can be added since, by nature of their infiniteness, the set includes all numbers—there is nothing to add. If this is hard to imagine, there is good reason: actual infinites do not exist and cannot exist in the physical world. If actual infinites did exist in the physical world, we would see absurdities and effects we could not live with, literally. For instance, let's say you had a CD collection that was infinitely large, and each CD had an infinite number of songs on it. If you listened to one CD, you hear as much music as if you had listened to all of the CDs—an infinite amount—and yet those infinites are of different sizes—a nonsensical notion. Let's also say that there were only two artists in your CD collection, Bach and the Beatles, and that every other CD was by the Beatles. This would mean that you had as many Beatles CDs as you would Beatles and Bach CDs combined; they would both be an infinite number. But at the same time they would be different sized infinites. And would the number of Beatles CDs be odd or even? It must be one or the other, but to speak of infinity in such a way is irrational."

"Or imagine a racecar driver and his son. The racecar driver is making circuit after circuit on a track a mile long. Meanwhile in the infield, his three-year-old son is on his tricycle going in circles. The son is completing a dozen or so circuits to his dad's one. But if they had each been going for an infinite amount of time, they would have completed an equal number of circuits! If this makes your brain hurt or is confusing at all, then you are beginning to understand why actual infinites do not exist in the physical world. These examples are not just interesting brainteasers or puzzles. The fact that if X = Y then X cannot also be twelve times greater than Y is extremely important. You would never want to cross a bridge, ride in a car, or live in a house designed by an engineer who didn't recognize or didn't care about the absurdities of actual infinites. This demonstration of the non-existence of actual infinites can be applied in two real-world areas, time and causality. The best way to show that time is not infinite, that it had a beginning, is to observe that there is a "now." If now exists, then time cannot be infinite. To show this, picture the moment "now" as a destination, like a train station. Then picture time as train tracks that are actually infinitely long. If you were a passenger waiting on the train to arrive, how long would you have to wait? The answer is: forever. You can never reach the end of infinity; thus, infinitely long train tracks cannot ever be crossed. There is no end to arrive at, no station. If infinitely long train tracks could be crossed, they would be the equivalent of a one-ended stick, a nonsensical notion. In fact, this is the opposite limitation of potential infinites. Just as potential infinites are finite numbers that can never turn infinite, actual infinites could never reach the end of their infiniteness and turn finite. But there is an end, a "now"; the train did arrive at the station. This means the tracks of time cannot be infinitely long. There cannot be an infinite number of preceding moments prior to the present moment. The past is not an actual infinite. Thus, time had to have a beginning. Time, however, did not cause itself to spring into existence. If it had a beginning, then something initiated it.

This is where causality comes into the picture. There is no such thing as an effect that was not caused. You are an effect of the biological process caused by your parents. These words you now read were caused by my typing on a keyboard. The current state of the universe is an effect caused by various astronomical and physical conditions. Note, however, that each of the causes mentioned are also effects. For example, your parents are not only your cause, but they are the effects of their parents who were the effects of their parents, and so on. But, as the non-existence of actual infinites shows, the chain of causes cannot regress forever. The train station in this case is made of present causes; because we have causes now, there must be a beginning to the sequence. Thus, there must be a cause that is not an effect, an uncaused cause, or first cause. Since the universe is an effect, it must have had a cause itself. The Kalam argument tells us that the universe had a beginning and that the beginning was caused by an uncaused cause. At this point there are only two options: either the cause was personal or it was impersonal. Reflection on what this uncaused cause would look like leads us to a conclusion rather quickly. The first cause would require an ability to create. Without this ability nothing could be created. It would also require an intention to create, a will to initiate the universe. Without this will to create, nothing would be created. It would require a non-contingent being, one whose existence depends on nothing but itself. If it was contingent, then it would simply be one more effect in the chain of causes and effects. And it must be transcendent. The cause of the universe must be outside of and apart from the universe. Now add all these things together. What kind of thing relies on nothing for its existence, has the power to create something from nothing, has a will to do it or not do it and has the characteristic of existing outside of the creation? Does this sound like a personal or impersonal being? Personal, of course. Thus, the Kalam argument brings us to the conclusion that the universe had a beginning that was caused by a personal, powerful, transcendent being." (Doug Powell, Holman QuickSource Guide to Christian Apologetics (Holman Quicksource Guides), 594-692 (Kindle Edition); Nashville, TN: Holman Reference)

Do you see the point?

An unlimited number of past lives of karmic debt would lead to an infinite regress, which is illogical and contradictory.

In the same way, an unlimited number of future lives of karmic debate would lead to an infinite regress.

This is another reason why Buddhism is illogical in regards to karma.

Fourth, the cycle of karma and samsara actually propagates the cycle of suffering in the world instead of solving it.

Hunt notes:

> "If a husband beats his wife, the cause-and-effect law of karma will cause him to be reincarnated in his next life as a wife who is beaten by her husband. That husband (who will have been prepared by his karma to be a wife-beater) must in turn come back in his next life as a wife beaten by her husband; a murderer must in turn become the victim of murder, and so forth endlessly. The perpetrator of each crime must become the victim of the same crime, which necessitates another perpetrator, who in turn must become a subsequent victim at the hands of yet another, ad infinitum. Rather than solving the problem of evil, karma and reincarnation perpetuate it." (Dave Hunt, Occult Invasion: The Subtle Seduction of the World and Church, 357-365 (Kindle Edition); Bend, OR; The Berean Call)

One former Buddhist monk, Tenzin Lahkpa (pseudonym) describes a debate he had with a well-known Buddhist monk, Tasha Lama, along these subjects. His words describe the biggest problem with the debt of mankind to God, Buddhism's faulty answer of karma, and how Jesus Christ is the only Solution to our dilemma.

"I wasn't clapping or allowing Tashi Lama to agree or disagree. The entire flow of my argument was unorthodox, but the argument itself was rudimentary. I knew that their patience toward me had already been worn thin because I had presented an open challenge to Tashi Lama, so I continued to push through with brevity. I could feel the audience hanging on my every word, ready to cheer for Tashi Lama when he "put me in my place." "This world that we exist in is the suffering-laden cycle of life, death, and rebirth without beginning or end. We wander from one life to another with no particular direction or purpose. Our life is characterized by dukkha—the unsatisfactory pain of a pointless life. Our only hope is to escape it all by working hard to obtain enough points to earn karma, which will propel us into nirvana—a state where suffering and existence cease." At this, I stomped my feet and clapped my hands together. My words were simple enough that every single person listening could follow along. Everything that I stated about Buddhism would have been thoroughly known by even the most uneducated person in the crowd. "Is this what you have called me out here to discuss in front of all these people, Tenzin? Do you need me to teach you the elementary subject of the Four Noble Truths?" Tashi Lama asked. The people laughed. "No, I have called you out here to ask, 'How do you know that the life-cycle is pointless? What if there is a purpose to suffering?'" The crowd went silent. During a debate, monks are supposed to make statements, not ask questions. "We spend our entire life suffering, and Buddha was supposed to illuminate the path that leads to the elimination of suffering, but who has escaped suffering by following the path? I would argue that we add to it. When we follow the path illuminated by the Buddha, we add to our own dukkha." The crowd gasped. "The entire merit-based system is exhausting! We are told to do so many things that lead to more suffering, and the additional suffering helps to accumulate merits that will contribute to the karma of the next life. We are commanded to stand, kneel, lay prostrate, spin wheels, chant, meditate, give offerings, give money, not eat, not marry, leave our family—the merit-earning never ends. Can suffering more lead to less suffering later on? After all of these years, I have to ask if our merit is enough to end suffering. What if we are not able to earn enough merit to end dukkha and experience nirvana? What if someone greater than we are is needed to end the suffering once and for all?" "Enough!" Tashi Lama said. "You are bringing judgment on us all by questioning the Buddha and offending the gods." "More judgment? You mean more than we already have? Look around at the suffering of our people. We are sick with no cure. We are hungry with no food. We are poor with no jobs. We are thirsty with no clean water. What have our merits earned us in heaven or on earth? Tashi Lama, I have seen you pray for hours and days and weeks. What have your prayers earned you? I have seen the people here spin prayer wheels until their arms could no longer be held up, and what mercy did they get?" "Stop him!" Tashi Lama yelled out. "Wait!" I held up my hand to delay the monks who were prepared to grab me. "Tashi Lama, what if I told you that there was a way to obtain merits that you did not earn?" Suddenly, the monks who were prepared to grab me waited to hear more…

"What if all of the merits that you have been trying to earn have already been earned and are now offered to you—not by works, but by grace?" There was a pause from Tashi Lama. "Om mani padme hummmmm," I chanted again and held out my hands in the chanting pose meant to channel the energy. "When we chant mantras, what are we doing? We are beckoning the aid of the spirit world to give us insight about something we do not understand—right? What if we need help from the spirit world not just to help with understanding, but to help with merit?" I felt that what I was saying was starting to make sense to everyone around me. I could tell that they were waiting for me to explain more to them. "What if I told you that I prayed to a God who said that He could guide me through the spirit world and I did not have to earn merits to hear from Him because He gave it all to me by grace. I could not earn it on my own." The

114

crowd was breathlessly silent. Not even prayer beads could be heard rolling through the rough knuckles of aged monks. "When I was lying in bed in the hospital, I was told about a God who gave His life for me so that I would not have to suffer dukkha any longer. He did not do it because I had earned enough merits. He did it because He loved me. His love leads to the path that ends suffering, and His name is Jesus." "Grab him now!" Tashi Lama shouted. "Kill him!" the crowd screamed. "He is a Christian! Kill him!" Suddenly, I was shoved to the ground and surrounded by several monks. My face was pushed into the dirt and I could feel the sharp jabs of feet kicking me in the ribs. I felt my hair being pulled. I hadn't shaved my head for a while and there was some growth on top, and the monks' hands were plucking at the stubble, but it wasn't giving them enough of a grip. Then someone latched their hands around my head and laced their fingers at the bottom of my chin and started to drag me backward across the dirt. I was choking and so I tried to propel myself with my feet in the direction that my head was being pulled, but there were too many people around. That is all I remember." (Tenzin Lahkpa & Eugene Bach, Leaving Buddha: A Tibetan Monk's Encounter with the Living God, 2996-3048 (Kindle Edition); New Kensington, Pa; Whitaker House)

Only the life and death of Jesus Christ may provide atonement for our sin.

Isaiah 64:6—But we are all like an unclean thing, And all our righteousnesses are like filthy rags; We all fade as a leaf, And our iniquities, like the wind, Have taken us away.

Romans 3:21-25 (Easy To Read Version)-But God has a way to make people right, and it has nothing to do with the law. He has now shown us that new way, which the law and the prophets told us about. (22) God makes people right through their faith in Jesus Christ. He does this for all who believe in Christ. Everyone is the same. (23) All have sinned and are not good enough to share God's divine greatness. (24) They are made right with God by his grace. This is a free gift. They are made right with God by being made free from sin through Jesus Christ. (25) God gave Jesus as a way to forgive people's sins through their faith in him. God can forgive them because the blood sacrifice of Jesus pays for their sins. God gave Jesus to show that he always does what is right and fair. He was right in the past when he was patient and did not punish people for their sins. And in our own time he still does what is right. God worked all this out in a way that allows him to judge people fairly and still make right any person who has faith in Jesus.

Romans 6:3-4—Or do you not know that as many of us as were baptized into Christ Jesus were baptized into His death? (4) Therefore we were buried with Him through baptism into death, that just as Christ was raised from the dead by the glory of the Father, even so we also should walk in newness of life.

Philippians 3:9—and be found in Him, not having my own righteousness, which is from the law, but that which is through faith in Christ, the righteousness which is from God by faith;

The grace of the Lord Jesus Christ, and the love of God, and the communion of the Holy Spirit, be with you all. Amen.

Questions

1. What are the Four Noble Truths?

　　_____
　　_____
　　_____

2. Give some examples of how an infinite regress is impossible.

　　_____
　　_____
　　_____
　　_____

3. What are some logical problems with panentheism?

_____

_____

_____

4. Provide a description of karma, along with some logical problems with the belief.

_____

_____

_____

_____

_____

5. Read Jon 9:1-3. How does the teaching of Jesus differ from the teaching of karma?

_____

_____

_____

6. Summarize the Doctrine Of Emanations.

_____

_____

_____

7. Read 2 Corinthians 5:14-21. How does the Gospel of Jesus Christ differ from the notion of karma?

_____

_____

_____

8. What are the main scriptures of Buddhism?

_____

9. What is Samsara? _____

10. What is the Buddha's real name?

_____

11. What was the name of the Buddha's son?

_____

12. At the birth of Buddha, there was a prophecy made about him to his father. What was it?

13. Do Buddhists claim to channel spirits? _____

14. What is the Eightfold Path?

15. What is another name for the Eightfold Path?

Lesson Five

Wicca (One)

One of the fastest growing religions in America is Wicca.

Sadly, however, there is a general lack of knowledge among many Christians regarding this religion, and as a direct result, many disciples of Christ are ill-equipped to reach out to their Wiccan friends.

In these lessons, we will examine some of the basic teachings and practices of Wicca, coupled with some suggestions for evangelism and witnessing to Wiccans.

The God And The Goddess Of Wicca

Wiccans typically believe in the ancient forms of paganism which existed before the Flood, including the concept that the universe itself was brought forth by two co-eternal forces, known to us today as "the god" and the "goddess." This is also known as "the Lord and the Lady." This system of belief is a mixture of two doctrines: pantheism and panentheism.

Pantheism is the belief that the entire universe is God, while panentheism is the teaching that the universe is the body of God which He inhabits and fills.

Wicca envisions that the original eternal Forces emptied themselves into the creation, and that therefore, the creation itself has become part of "God." There are numerous problems with both pantheism and panentheism (see Lesson Three of this series for a more detailed explanation).

119

A Closer Look at the Lord and the Lady in Wicca

Wicca teaches that the original energy that formed the God and the Goddess has descended into the universe itself, and that this energy can be harnessed through the practice of ritualistic magic.

Furthermore, through the belief in reincarnation (i.e., the continual birth and rebirth of individuals over the vast eons of time) it is held that a person can ascend to higher levels of consciousness and become "gods" or "goddesses" as a result of their various incarnations. This is very similar to Hindu teaching regarding karma and reincarnation.

In describing the Wiccan concept of the God and the Goddess, one Wiccan explains:

> "ALL RELIGIONS ARE structures built upon reverence of deity. Wicca is no exception. The Wicca acknowledge a supreme divine power, unknowable, ultimate, from which the entire universe sprang. The concept of this power, far beyond our comprehension, has nearly been lost in Wicca because of our difficulty in relating to it. Wiccans, however, link with this force through their deities. In accordance with the principles of nature, the supreme power was personified into two basic beings: the Goddess and the God....Because the Wicca see deity inherent in nature, many of us are involved in ecology—saving the earth from utter destruction by our own hands. The Goddess and God still exist, as they have always existed, and to honor them we honor and preserve our precious planet. In Wiccan thought, the deities didn't exist before our spiritual ancestor's acknowledgement of them. However, the energies behind them did; they created us. Early worshippers recognized these forces as the Goddess and God, personifying them in an attempt to understand them. The Old Ones didn't die when the ancient pagan religions fell to Christianity in Europe. Most of the rites vanished, but they weren't the only effective ones. Wicca is alive and well and the deities respond to our calls and invocations. When envisioning the Goddess and God, many of the Wicca see them as well-

known deities from ancient religions. Diana, Pan, Isis, Hermes, Hina, Tammuz, Hecate, Ishtar, Cerridwen, Thoth, Tara, Aradia, Artemis, Pélé, Apollo, Kanaloa, Bridget, Helios, Bran, Lugh, Hera, Cybele, Inanna, Maui, Ea, Athena, Lono, Marduk—the list is virtually endless. Many of these deities, with their corresponding histories, rites, and mythic information, furnish the concept of deity for Wiccans....

"The Goddess and God are equal; neither is higher or more deserving of respect. Though some Wiccans focus their rituals toward the Goddess and seem to forget the God entirely, this is a reaction to centuries of stifling patriarchal religion, and the loss of acknowledgement of the feminine aspect of divinity. Religion based entirely on feminine energy, however, is as unbalanced and unnatural as one totally masculine in focus. The ideal is a perfect balance of the two. The Goddess and God are equal, complementary....

"Since the Goddess is nature, all nature, she is both the temptress and the crone; the tornado and the fresh spring rain; the cradle and the grave....

"The Goddess has been known as the Queen of Heaven, Mother of the Gods that Made the Gods, the Divine Source, the Universal Matrix, the Great Mother, and by countless other titles....

"The God has been revered for eons. He is neither the stern, all-powerful deity of Christianity and Judaism, nor is he simply the consort of the Goddess. God or Goddess, they are equal, one....

"With the Goddess, he also celebrates and rules sex. The Wicca don't avoid sex or speak of it in hushed words. It's a part of nature and is accepted as such. Since it brings pleasure, shifts our awareness away from the everyday world, and perpetuates our species, it is thought to be sacred. The God lustily imbues us with the urge that ensures our species 'biological future....

"Of old, the God was the Sky Father, and the Goddess, the Earth Mother. The God of the sky, of rain and lightning, descended upon and united with the Goddess, spreading seed upon the land, celebrating her fertility. Today the deities of Wicca are still firmly associated with fertility, but every aspect of human existence can be linked with the Goddess and God. They can be called upon to help us sort through the vicissitudes of our existences and bring joy into our often spiritually bereft lives....

"Beyond this, the Goddess and God can help us change our lives. Because the deities are the creative forces of the universe (not just symbols), we can call upon them to empower our rites and to bless our magic. Again, this is in direct opposition to most religions. The power is in the hands of every practitioner, not specialized priests or priestesses who perform these feats for the masses. This is what makes Wicca a truly satisfying way of life. We have direct links with the deities. No intermediaries are needed; no priests or confessors or shamans. We are the shamans." (Scott Cunningham, *Wicca: A Guide For The Solitary Practitioner,* 226-320 (Kindle Edition); Woodbury, MN: Llewellyn Publications)

The Wiccan will usually therefore acknowledge belief in the "God" or the "Goddess," and will at the same time acknowledge that the existence of all the gods and goddesses of the religions around the world is possible and (in many cases), probable.

God As Both Male And Female

Wiccans teach that the original Creator is both male and female. This is something which Christians and Wiccans may find agreement on, at least in principle. While the Bible teaches that God is neither male nor female (literally), it also teaches that He manifests as both male and female (representatively).

"With this basic understanding of the nature of gender, it seems apparent that God, having neither a sexed body nor a human culture, cannot have a gender. Yet does the testimony of Scripture support this conclusion? Although the Bible often speaks of God in masculine terms and even figuratively describes Him as having body parts, God is never said to have reproductive organs (as Baal and other gods had). God has no female god as a counterpart, and He does not produce the world through procreation, but through His spoken word. Moreover, John 4:24 testifies, "God is spirit." An implication of this verse is that God, being holy and transcendent, has no body and exists as a being wholly outside the realm of creaturely existence. Because sexuality and gender are characteristics of bodily creatures, God cannot have gender. Moreover, some Bible texts specifically warn against identifying God with human males and females. Numbers 23:19 warns that "God is not a man [ish: male human], that He should lie, nor a son of man [adam: human], that He should repent" (NASB). Hosea 11:9 is similar: "I am God and not man [ish], the Holy One in your midst." In speaking of the righteous nature of God's character, both texts prohibit thinking of God as a man. The clearest teaching on this subject is found in Deuteronomy 4:15-16: "So watch yourselves carefully, since you did not see any form on the day the LORD spoke to you at Horeb from the midst of the fire, so that you do not act corruptly and make a graven image for yourselves in the form of any figure, the likeness of male or female" (NASB). In this way, imaging God as male or female is considered idolatry, suggesting strongly that the biblical tradition is against attributing gender to God. Despite the fact that Scripture often uses language for God that is suitable for a masculine person, God is not like a human male in His form or character." (Ed Hindson & Ergun Caner, *The Popular Encyclopedia Of Apologetics,* 244-245 (Kindle Edition); Eugene, Oregon; Harvest House Publishers)

Does The Bible View Women Negatively?

It is here that we need to consider another stereotype about Christianity in the Wiccan belief system: the status of women. It is commonly believed that women are marginalized and devalued in the Christian Scriptures. They are perhaps unaware of the ways that the Bible actually teaches the equality of women and men.

Notice that in the Creation we are told about the equality of male and female from the very beginning:

> *Genesis 1:26-27—Then God said, "Let Us make man in Our image, according to Our likeness; let them have dominion over the fish of the sea, over the birds of the air, and over the cattle, over all the earth and over every creeping thing that creeps on the earth." (27) So God created man in His own image; in the image of God He created him; male and female He created them.*

According to the Bible, God created men and women to be equal.

Later, we are told that God commanded children to honor both father and mother equally:

> *Exodus 20:12—Honor your father and your mother, that your days may be long upon the land which the LORD your God is giving you.*

in the New Testament, we see more examples of God elevating and honoring women through the work of His Son and Apostles.

For example, the very first eyewitness to Jesus' resurrection from the dead was a woman:

> *Mark 16:9—Now when He rose early on the first day of the week, He appeared first to Mary Magdalene, out of whom He had cast seven demons.*

This is amazing when we consider how women were treated in first century Judaism, particularly in regard to legal testimony in courts of law:

> "Sooner let the words of the Law be burnt than delivered to women." (Talmud, Sotah 19a)

"The world cannot exist without males and without females-happy is he whose children are males, and woe to him whose children are females. (Talmud, Kiddushin 82b)

"But let not the testimony of women be admitted, on account of the levity and boldness of their sex, nor let servants be admitted to give testimony on account of the ignobility of their soul; since it is probable that they may not speak truth, either out of hope of gain, or fear of punishment. (Josephus, Antiquities 4.8.15)

"Any evidence which a woman [gives] is not valid (to offer), also they are not valid to offer. This is equivalent to saying that one who is Rabbinically accounted a robber is qualified to give the same evidence as a woman. (Talmud, Rosh Hashannah 1.8)

On a side note, this also teaches us something regarding the credibility of the Apostles report regarding the resurrection of Christ from the dead (1 Corinthians 15:1-8).

"4. The naming of specific women as the first witnesses to the empty tomb was highly embarrassing for the first-century Jews. A woman's testimony was considered as practically worthless in a court of law and was hardly ever allowed. No invented account would have named any women as the first witnesses if it wanted to gain credibility. Moreland notes, "This probably explains why the women are not mentioned in 1 Corinthians 15 and the speeches of Acts, since these speeches were evangelistic." (MoJP.S 168) Further, that Mary Magdalene (one previously possessed by demons) is named would have further eroded confidence in the report. The only possible reason for a writer including this information is that he was compelled to tell the truth, the whole truth and nothing but the truth." (Josh McDowell & Bill Wilson, Evidence For The Historical Jesus: A Compelling Case For His Life And His Claims, 6774-6778 (Kindle Edition); Eugene, Oregon; Harvest House Publishers)

More to the point, the fact that Jesus chose a woman to be the first eyewitness of His resurrection demonstrates the attitude towards women that Jesus and His followers had.

Consider another example from the life of Jesus

> *Luke 10:38-42—Now it happened as they went that He entered a certain village; and a certain woman named Martha welcomed Him into her house. (39) And she had a sister called Mary, who also sat at Jesus' feet and heard His word. (40) But Martha was distracted with much serving, and she approached Him and said, "Lord, do You not care that my sister has left me to serve alone? Therefore tell her to help me." (41) And Jesus answered and said to her, "Martha, Martha, you are worried and troubled about many things. (42) But one thing is needed, and Mary has chosen that good part, which will not be taken away from her.*

Notice that Mary was a woman who "sat at Jesus' feet." This was a Jewish expression that meant that Mary was a recognized disciple of Jesus, being taught His Word as male disciples were also. In the first century world of Judaism, this was amazing!

> "One very familiar story in Luke's account is that of Mary and Martha (Luke 10:38–42). Preachers often pose the question, "Which are you, Mary or Martha?" in sermons. This is an excellent teaching passage on taking the time to learn and be contemplative. In Luke 10:39, however, Mary is sitting at the feet of Jesus. This was the position that a disciple took. It's the very same posture that Paul took when he learned from Gamaliel in Jerusalem (Acts 22:3; cf. Luke 8:35). What's so startling about this story is that women were not disciples of rabbis. Period! They received no formal education, and the only skills they were taught were typically household duties. Moreover, if a man instructed his daughter in the Law, it was as if he was teaching her lustfulness according to the rabbis (m. Sotah 3.4). Women were too simple minded to learn such deep truths, so it was believed. For Mary to have become a disciple was for Jesus to have elevated women. This one small detail in this story

126

is often overlooked, but it is a profound truth in a short phrase. Luke shows that Christ elevated women to the status of a disciple (Luke 24:10)." (Steven Hunter, Being Phoebe: How Women Served in Early Christianity (Start2Finish Bible Studies), 13 (Kindle Edition); Dallas, TX; Start2Finish Books)

When we look at the way that Jesus treated women in the first century, we can understand why so many adore Him.

"JESUS'S CHARACTER

- Loyal
- Trustworthy
- Honest
- Moral
- Attentive
- The highest level of integrity
- Direct
- Smart
- Supportive
- Faithful
- A gentleman
- Respects you
- Emotionally intelligent
- He is willing to put the work in to get you where you need to be
- Will never leave you
- Will never condemn you
- Wants only the best for you
- Has your back
- The best friend you'll ever have
- Best big brother ever And above all
- Is crazy stinkin' in love with you and wants you to follow Him wholeheartedly.

No, you didn't just time warp and open up a Glamour Magazine to a checklist touting all the best qualities of a perfect mate. Do you see? Do you understand? These women in this book might not all be like you, but I know there's at least one you can relate to. These women were flesh and bone like us: flawed, bent and most likely their own worst enemies. Can you hear some of the self-talk? Jesus lovingly met each where they were and was gracious enough not to leave them there. With patience, commitment, unconditional love, and acceptance He's holding out His hand to you now to do the same." (Dawn Baggott Ford, Jesus's Stops: The women Jesus encountered in John's gospel and why it matters now, 39 (Kindle Edition); Maitland, FL; Xulon Press)

Observe further that the Apostle Paul allowed women to be taught alongside the male disciples in the first century:

1 Timothy 2:11—Let a woman learn in silence with all submission.

This again speaks to the positive influence of Christianity in the world towards women.

"Concerning the question of educating women in the Church, however, much is known. Whenever Paul established a church, he insisted that women were to be educated in the faith. He began this passage in 1 Timothy with the words "let a woman learn," and while such a program would be in keeping with Paul's goal for women, it was at variance with Jewish and Greek customs. Jewish women were not included in formal education. It was permissible for a man to teach Scripture to both boys and girls, 1 but a woman could not teach even the youngest of children in a school, and one rabbi said that "if a man gives his daughter a knowledge of the Law, it is as though he taught her lechery." Women were to be educated only in matters regarding homemaking skills. As one rabbi said, "There is no wisdom in woman except with the distaff." (See chapter 1, this volume.)...

"Therefore, Paul's desire that women be educated in the faith was both radical in thought and difficult in execution. Women were not used to listening to lectures or thinking about theological concepts, or studying at all....

128

"But the word for silence is a lovely word, hesuchia (hey-soo-KEY-ah). It does not mean simply refraining from talking. It means restful quietness, as in meditation or study. A few sentences before, Paul used this same word to describe the peaceful and quiet life (1 Tim. 2:2), good and acceptable before God, the kind of life Paul wished for all believers....It is quite possible that Paul had in mind a certain woman or group of women in Ephesus when he wrote this passage. If so, Paul was not willing to lessen his insistence that women are to learn, in spite of the high-handed attitude of one or some. Instead, he wrote that they are to learn in quietness, without being rude or domineering." (John Temple Bristow, What Paul Really Said About Women: The Apostle's Liberating Views on Equality in Marriage, Leadership, and Love, 70-72 (Kindle Edition, emphasis added); New York, NY; HarperCollins NY).

Sometimes people believe that the God of the Bible devalues women because they misunderstand passages like this one in Leviticus:

Then the LORD spoke to Moses, saying, (2) "Speak to the children of Israel, saying: 'If a woman has conceived, and borne a male child, then she shall be unclean seven days; as in the days of her customary impurity she shall be unclean. (3) And on the eighth day the flesh of his foreskin shall be circumcised. (4) She shall then continue in the blood of her purification thirty-three days. She shall not touch any hallowed thing, nor come into the sanctuary until the days of her purification are fulfilled. (5) 'But if she bears a female child, then she shall be unclean two weeks, as in her customary impurity, and she shall continue in the blood of her purification sixty-six days. (Leviticus 12:1-5)

Here, the Bible tells us that if a woman in Israel gave birth to a boy, she would be unclean for a period of thirty-three days. However, if she had a female baby, she would be unclean for sixty-six days.

Is this an example of the Bible paying special treatment towards males, while at the same time devaluing women?

When we look carefully here, we see that God is actually displaying His love and care for women!

Years ago, one doctor investigated the matter thoroughly and was amazed to find how modern science actually demonstrates ways that this passage of Scripture safeguards the life of the mother who has given birth:

"The writer became interested in the passage quoted above in connection with experimental research he and his assistants have conducted on the effects of drugs and toxins on living plant protoplasm...

"The material examined was serum obtained from blood specimens drawn from 'come-back' patients of the Lying-In Department of the Women's Clinic, John Hopkins Hospital. In this clinic, as a routine procedure, every maternity case is required to return for a complete examination six weeks after the birth of the child. The author endeavored to obtain specimens from as many of such 'come-back' patients in good health as possible. A total number of 223 blood specimens from as many patients were examined...

"What is of greater interest in the present connection is the fact that there was a distinct difference in the toxicity of puerperal blood specimens obtained from six weeks after delivery in respect to sex of the offspring. The average of all readings obtained from blood specimens procured after female births revealed that these were more toxic than those obtained after male births. These results are not altogether surprising. It is quite possible that blood obtained after childbirth may show differences dependent on the sex of the offspring. Within the last few years it has been demonstrated by the Russian investigator Manoiloff, and by others repeating and extending his work, that certain chemical differences between the blood of male and female animals and, indeed, between the extracts of male and female plants, can be detected by suitable methods. It is therefore possible that blood obtained from women who have given birth to male children may show chemical and biological differences from blood obtained from mothers bearing female offspring. The present findings certainly speak in favor of such a view and throw an interesting light on the Biblical passage which is the subject of the present paper. It seems entirely possible that observation of the relative danger involved for the male in the resumption of intercourse, danger inherent in the relative toxicity of the post-puerperal blood conditions in the female, is responsible for the distinction between the duration of a woman's impurity after the birth of male and female children. Moreover, it is interesting to note that this scientific basis for the Biblical distinction between the two sexes after childbirth is in complete agreement with the most orthodox Hebrew commentators on the Bible." (David I. Macho, 'A Scientific Appreciation Of Leviticus 12:1-5,' in *The Journal Of Biblical Literature* (Volume 52; Number 4-December, 1933); 2-9).

More recently, another doctor has written:

"When a woman had a male child she was excluded from the sanctuary for 33 days and for a female child 66 days. Was this an arbitrary ruling by God? Before we get into that, let's look at childbirth in general. Back in the days the Torah was written, infant mortality rates were much higher than they are today (and they still remain high in some parts of the world). The mother's immune system is depressed at childbirth from the stress of the birth and hormonal changes, and needs some time to recover and build up immunity. The last thing she needs is to go into an environment where they are slaughtering animals and there is a buildup of infectious organisms. The baby's immune system is also suppressed. The reason for this is that babies are born with more or less sterile intestinal tracts. Growing the correct intestinal flora is critical for proper digestion, immune function, etc. A short list of what the gut flora accomplishes is as follows:

Help kill harmful microbes that get into your intestine through eating contaminated food. Stimulate lymphoid tissue to make antibodies to pathogens. Decrease allergies by increasing oral tolerance to certain foods. Help in the synthesis of certain B vitamins, as well as magnesium, calcium and iron. Help regulate body weight and prevent obesity. Metabolize ingested carcinogens. Increases the body's absorption of water. Helps proper carbohydrate digestion and fermentation. If the baby's immune system was very active it would attack the colonizing intestinal bacteria and the baby would not colonize the right microbes that are fostered by nursing. It takes approximately 5-6 weeks for this process to occur. This discovery has only been solidified in science since 2013. God knew way before that and protected mother and baby by keeping them isolated. But why do they stay away for twice as long if they have a female child? Since 1979, scientists have been aware of a phenomena called fetomaternal microchimerism. What this term means is that after childbirth they still find some Y chromosomes (females have two X chromosomes while males have an X and a Y) still in the mother. Some theories suggest that the mother's body treats them as a foreign invader and ramps up the immune system to try to deal with them. That being the case, a mother's immunity will recover quicker if she has a male child, as opposed to having a female child, and she can return to normal functions sooner without putting her or her baby's health at risk. God thus protects the mother with this commandment by giving her the correct amount of time to "recover"." (Dr. Michael Lebowitz, God's Preventative Medicine: New Scientific Discoveries Validate Biblical Instructions, 108-109 (Kindle Edition); MZBooks)

Sometimes people claim that women in the Old Testament were regarded by the God of the Bible as property of men. After all, some argue, doesn't the presence of the drowsy in the Old Testament mean that women were just something to be bought off and sold?

Not at all!

Speaking of the dowry in the Old Testament, Copan has pointed out:

> "The idea of bride-price is presented by the New Atheists as though it's a matter of buying a wife like you would a horse or a mule. In actual fact, the bride-price was the way a man showed his serious intentions toward his bride-to-be, and it was a way of bringing two families together to discuss a serious, holy, and lifelong matter. Having sex with a young woman without the necessary preparations and formal ceremony cheapened the woman and sexuality. The process surrounding the bride-price reflected the honorable state of marriage. Think of the dowry system used in places like India. In this case, the family of the bride-to-be gives money to the future husband's family. Such a transaction hardly means that the groom-to-be is mere property! Why automatically conclude that a woman is property because this marriage gift is given in the Old Testament but that a man isn't property under the dowry system? The bride-price was more like a deposit from the groom's father to the bride's father. The Hebrew word for this deposit (mohar) is better translated "marriage gift." It not only helped create closer family ties between the two families but also provided economic stability for a marriage. This gift given to the bride's father (often several years 'worth of wages) compensated him for the work his daughter would otherwise have contributed to the family. The marriage gift— preserved by the husband throughout the marriage—also served as security for the wife in case of divorce or her husband's death. 9 In fact, the bride's father would often give an even larger gift of property when the couple married. Hitchens's complaint about the Old Testament's bride-price is misguided." (Paul Copan, Is God a Moral Monster?: Making Sense of the Old Testament God, 117 (Kindle Edition); Grand Rapids, Michigan; Baker Books)

Careful study reveals that the Bible elevates women.

Interestingly enough, this was quite different from the way that women were regarded in other cultures and religions from the ancient world.

"A respectable Athenian woman was not permitted to leave her house unless she was accompanied by a trustworthy male escort, commonly a slave appointed by her husband. When the husband's male guests were present in his home, she was not permitted to eat or interact with them. She had to retire to her woman's quarters (gynaeceum). The only woman who had some freedom was the hetaera, or mistress, who often accompanied a married man when he attended events outside his home. The hetaera was the man's companion and sexual partner. The Greek wife had virtually no freedom. Even in Sparta, where women had more freedom than in Athens, men kept their wives "under lock and key," according to Plutarch, the second-century Greek biographer and essayist (Lycurgus 15.8). The poet Aristophanes has Calonice say in one of his plays, "We women can't go out just when we like. We have to wait upon our men" (Lysistrata 16–19). The average Athenian woman had the social status of a slave. And according to Euripides ' tragedy Medea, the wife could not divorce her husband, whereas he could divorce her anytime. Small wonder that Medea in Euripides 'play lamented, "Surely, of all creatures that have life and wit, we women are of all unhappiest" (Medea 231–32). Greek discrimination against women began early in a woman's life cycle. Nonslave boys in Athens were sent to school, "taught to read and write, and educated in poetry, music and gymnastics; girls did not go to school at all," says one Greek scholar. Throughout a woman's entire life she was not permitted to speak in public. Sophocles wrote, "O woman, silence is an adornment to woman" (Ajax 293); Euripides asserted, "Silence and discretion are most beautiful in woman, and remaining quiet within the house" (Heraclitus 476); and the philosopher Aristotle said, "Silence gives grace to woman" (Politics 1.1260a). But long before the days of Euripides, Sophocles, and Aristophanes, the writer Homer portrayed Telemachus

134

rebuking his mother Penelope for speaking in the presence of men. Dogmatically, he tells her that "speech shall be for men" (Odyssey 1.359). The Athenian woman was also deemed inferior to man. Given this cultural perception, the Greek poets were fond of equating her with evil. Euripides (480–406 B.C.) has Hippolytus ask, "Why hast thou given a home beneath the sun, Zeus, unto woman, specious curse to man?" (Hippolytus 616–17). Aeschylus (525?–456 B.C.) has a chorus declare, "Evil of mind are they [women], and guileful of purpose, with impure hearts" (Suppliant Maidens 748–49). Another Greek poet, Aristophanes, has the chorus in his play Lysistrata say, "For women are a shameless set, the vilest of creatures going" (368–69). The great epic writer Homer has Agamemnon declare, "One cannot trust women" (Odyssey 11). And, of course, it was the Greek myth of Pandora's jar that blamed woman for introducing evil into the world." (Alvin J. Schmidt, How Christianity Changed the World, 98-99 (Kindle Edition, emphasis added, M.T.); Grand Rapids, Michigan; Zondervan)

When we consider these facts, it is little surprise that scholars throughout time have recognized the amazing impact of Christianity on recognizing the equality of women with men.

"One scholar of ancient Rome has aptly said that "the conversion of the Roman world to Christianity [brought] a great change in woman's status." Another has expressed it even more succinctly: "The birth of Jesus was the turning point in the history of woman."" (Alvin J. Schmidt, How Christianity Changed the World, 98 (Kindle Edition); Grand Rapids, Michigan; Zondervan)

Protecting The Planet

Wiccans are very well known for their belief in sustaining the planet. This is due in large part to their religious belief that the universe is an extension of God. Indeed, this is also another area where Christians and Wiccans may find common ground.

Notice what the Bible tells us:

Genesis 1:28—Then God blessed them, and God said to them, "Be fruitful and multiply; fill the earth and subdue it; have dominion over the fish of the sea, over the birds of the air, and over every living thing that moves on the earth."

The Bible here teaches that God expects mankind to "subdue" the Earth. The word used here has reference to caring for and exploring the Earth. This is reinforced by other Scriptures which teach that God created mankind to be a steward of the Earth.

Psalm 8:6—You have made him to have dominion over the works of Your hands; You have put all things under his feet,

We learn:

"In Psalm 8:6, the original Hebrew word used for "rule" is mashal. It indicates that Adam was God's manager here, God's steward or governor. Adam was God's mediator, go-between or representative. Psalm 115:16 confirms this: "The heaven... the Eternal holds himself, the earth He has assigned to men" (Moffatt, emphasis added). God didn't give away ownership of the earth, but He did assign the responsibility of governing it to humanity....

"Now, it's no small task to re-present God. So to help humans carry out this assignment, God made us so much like Himself that it was scary. "And God created man in His own image, in the image of God He created him; male and female He created them" (Gen. 1:27). The Hebrew word for "image" is tselem, which involves the concept of a "shadow," a "phantom" or an "Illusion.," An illusion is something you think you see, but on closer observation you discover that your eyes have tricked you. When the rest of creation saw Adam, they must've done a double take: Man, I could've sworn I saw God—oh, it's just Adam. How's that for re-presentation? We're also told that Adam was similar to or comparable to God. The Hebrew word demuwth, translated "likeness" in Genesis 1:26, comes from the root word damah, meaning "to compare." Adam was very much like God! Psalm 8:5 actually says human beings were made just "a little lower than God" and that we were crowned with

136

God's very own glory. The definition of the Hebrew word kabowd that's translated "glory" literally means "heavy or weighty" !6 It's linked to the concept of authority. We still use the picture today when we refer to someone who "carries a lot of weight." Adam carried God's weight on the earth. I don't know what Adam weighed but he was heavy. He represented God with full authority! He was large and in charge! The Greek word for glory, doxa, is just as loaded. It involves the concept of recognition. More specifically, it's what causes someone (or something) to be recognized for who he or she (or it) really is. When we read in Scripture that humankind is the glory of God (see 1 Cor. 11:7), it's telling us that God was recognized in humans. Why? So humans could accurately represent Him. When creation looked at Adam, they were supposed to see God. And they did! That is, until Adam sinned and couldn't carry the weight of God's glory anymore." (Dutch Sheets, *Getting In God's Face: How Prayer Really Works,* 16-18 (Kindle Edition); Ventura, CA; Regal)

We are called on by God to care for this planet.

"If we abusively exploit God's creation for the sake of our own self-interest, we will not escape final accountability. Consider John's warning: "Your wrath has come, and the time for judging the dead, for rewarding Your servants, the prophets and the saints and who fear Your name, both small and great, and for destroying those who destroy the earth" (Rev. 11:18; emphasis ours). As God rules over us, we expect goodness and fairness and for God to continually do what is in humanity's best interests. Therefore, if we count upon God's benevolent rule, why would we ever presume God would approve humanity's abusive, self-serving reign over creation? Exploitive misuse (Ezek. 34:18–19) and wastefulness (John 6:12) are unseemly in God's eyes. Genesis 9:12–13 testifies to God's love and faithfulness toward creation, which God expects humanity to share: "This is the sign of the covenant that I make between Me and you and every living creature that is with you, for all future generations: I have set my bow in the clouds, and it shall be a sign of the covenant between Me and the earth" (Gen. 9:12–13). God has covenanted with the earth and its life. Consequently, humans, formed in his likeness, must exercise responsible care in ruling what clearly belongs to God....Christians value and love creation because God loves it and intends to redeem it alongside humanity. Those who describe God as only caring about humanity are not describing the God revealed in Scripture. The earth and its resources were created by God and declared valuable ("very good") independent of human utility. Deuteronomy 22:6–7 is one of my favorite biblical texts advocating creation care: If you come on a bird's nest, in any tree or on the ground, with fledglings or eggs, with the mother sitting on the fledglings or on the eggs, you shall not take the mother with the young. Let the mother go, taking only the young for yourself, in order that it may go well with you and you may live long. When I took my first wildlife management class in college, the professor said something astonishing that I had never heard before. This Deuteronomic prescription is the oldest known written law about wildlife conservation. In effect, God charged ancient Israel with game warden responsibilities. And there are other examples. In Exodus it says, "But the seventh year you shall let [the crop field] rest and lie fallow, so that the poor of your people may eat; and what they leave the wild animals may eat. You shall do the same with your vineyard, and with your olive orchard" (23:11). In Leviticus it says, "When you reap the harvest of your land, you shall not reap to the very edges of your field, or gather the gleanings of your harvest" (19:9). Conservation practices—mandated in the Torah—benefited land, people, and wildlife. We have similar agricultural programs in the United States, which pay farmers to leave portions of their crop fields unplanted (fallow) or unharvested to increase soil fertility and to provide food and cover for wildlife. In another passage, God expects those who prosecute wars to protect trees: If you besiege a town for a long time, making war against it in

138

order to take it, you must not destroy its trees by wielding an ax against them. Although you may take food from them, you must not cut them down. Are trees in the field human beings that they should come under siege from you? (Deut. 20:19) If ancient warriors were responsible for executing their plans in a conservationist manner, there is little doubt what God might think about modern technological warfare whose collateral damage often results in widespread despoliation of the land." (John Mark Hicks, Bobby Valentine, & and Mark Wilson, *EMBRACING CREATION God's Forgotten Mission*, 2063-2097 (Kindle Edition); Abilene, TX; Abilene Christian University Press)

The grace of the Lord Jesus Christ, and the love of God, and the communion of the Holy Spirit, be with you all. Amen.

Questions

1. What are some reasons why so many people are embracing Wicca in our country today?

   _____

   _____

2. What does the Hebrew word mashal mean?

   _____

   _____

3. List some Bible verses which shows that women were loved and highly regarded by God.

   _____

   _____

   _____

4. List some Scriptures where God says He is literally without gender.

   _____

   _____

   _____

5. Who are the "God" and the "Goddess" in Wiccan belief?

   _____

_____
_____
_____

6. How were women often regarded in the ancient pagan
   religions and cultures? List some specific examples.

_____
_____
_____
_____
_____

7. What are some evidences from the Bible that God expects
   mankind to care for the universe that He has made?

_____
_____
_____
_____
_____

8. What did Paul mean when he said that women should learn in
   "silence?"

_____
_____
_____

Lesson Six

Wicca (Two)

Origins Of Wicca

In our last lesson, we learned that Wiccans hold to a panentheistic belief system. Believing that the original creative force descended into the universe, they believe in the "Lord" and the "Lady." These are often referred to as the "God" and the "Goddess."

Wiccans often refer to the Goddess as the Queen of Heaven.

This is interesting terminology that may be reflected in the Bible.

The Prophet Jeremiah wrote:

> *Jeremiah 7:18—The children gather wood, the fathers kindle the fire, and the women knead dough, to make cakes for the queen of heaven; and they pour out drink offerings to other gods, that they may provoke Me to anger.*

> *Jeremiah 44:17-19—But we will certainly do whatever has gone out of our own mouth, to burn incense to the queen of heaven and pour out drink offerings to her, as we have done, we and our fathers, our kings and our princes, in the cities of Judah and in the streets of Jerusalem. For then we had plenty of food, were well-off, and saw no trouble. (18) But since we stopped burning incense to the queen of heaven and pouring out drink offerings to her, we have lacked everything and have been consumed by the sword and by famine." (19) The women also said, "And when we burned incense to the queen of heaven and poured out drink offerings to her, did we make cakes for her, to worship her, and pour out drink offerings to her without our husbands' permission?"*

Jeremiah 44:25—Thus says the LORD of hosts, the God of Israel, saying: 'You and your wives have spoken with your mouths and fulfilled with your hands, saying, "We will surely keep our vows that we have made, to burn incense to the queen of heaven and pour out drink offerings to her." You will surely keep your vows and perform your vows!'

Jeremiah spoke here of a pagan goddess and her worshippers. As we will learn, there are powerful indicators of the origin of Wicca.

Simon The Sorcerer

Many researchers believe that the origin of Wicca is tied in directly with a man in the Bible known as Simon the Sorcerer (or Simon Magus).

We are first introduced to Simon in the Book of Acts:

Acts 8:9-13—But there was a certain man called Simon, who previously practiced sorcery in the city and astonished the people of Samaria, claiming that he was someone great, (10) to whom they all gave heed, from the least to the greatest, saying, "This man is the great power of God." (11) And they heeded him because he had astonished them with his sorceries for a long time. (12) But when they believed Philip as he preached the things concerning the kingdom of God and the name of Jesus Christ, both men and women were baptized. (13) Then Simon himself also believed; and when he was baptized he continued with Philip, and was amazed, seeing the miracles and signs which were done.

Simon, unfortunately, soon apostatized from the Christian faith and was soundly rebuked by the Apostle Peter, even as he was exhorted to repent and pray to the Lord for forgiveness (Acts 8:14-22). Church history, however, reports that Simon continued in his wickedness, incorporating various forms of paganism with the teaching of the Apostles.

In essence, Simon Magus became one of the first Gnostics.

Who Are The Gnostics?

The Gnostics were a group of people who began to spring up in the late century church. They attempted to combine Christianity and pagan religion together.

Johnson provides a basic description of some major Gnostic teachings:

"The basic teachings of Gnosticism that the church called heresy are: There are thirty Aeons (gods) that exist in the Pleroma, outside time and space. The goddess, Sophia, created the Demiurge, a creator angel (the god of the Old Testament) who was a tyrant; and being unaware of the Aeons, thought he was the only God. He created man; but Sophia gave man a spirit. Some may be saved if they do enough good works; but some are predestined to go to hell. (works salvation) Gnostics have spirits that are emanations from Sophia. This makes them predestined to be saved. It is imposable for them to lose their salvation. It does not matter if their behavior is good or evil. The most " perfect " of them addict themselves to evil deeds and are in a habit of defiling the women they convert. Eventually all matter will be destroyed since matter is evil and not capable of salvation. Gnostics will become spirits and will marry the angels. Christ descended upon Jesus at His baptism and left before Jesus went before Pilate. Sophia would not allow Christ to suffer. (Adoptionism) They utter mantras to effect nature. (Hindu mantra and Kabalistic letter magic, Gramera, and emanations) Souls reincarnate. Perfect knowledge is obtained by baptism, spiritual marriage, and last rites. (Sacramentalism) Sophia sent the serpent (the angel Michael or Samael) into the Garden of Eden to free Eve and Adam. By eating from the tree they attained true Gnosis and were set free. Sophia saved Noah from the flood sent by the evil Demiurge. The Demiurge forced Eve into sexual intercourse many times. Eve thereby gave birth to other evil creator angels. (Serpent Seed)." (Ken Johnson, *Ancient Church Fathers: What The Disciples Of The Apostles Taught,* 165-166 (Kindle Edition))

Let's notice some of the major Gnostics and Gnostic groups.

Chart Of Prominent Gnostics And Gnostic Groups

Simon Magus	The sorcerer of Acts 8, Simon was a Christian who left the faith. Church history declares that he was the founder of the Gnostic movement. He is noted for exorcisms, love-potions, incantations and spells, the use of familiar spirits called Paradri, and dream-senders called Oniropompi. Some evidence suggests that Simon was also the founder of the religion known today as Wicca.
Menander	Disciple of Simon Magus. Through the use of sorcery, you will be able to overcome the angels who made the universe. You must be baptized into Menander to one day obtain the resurrection and remain forever young.
Ebionites	Founded by Ebion. God created the world; Jesus was just a good man. Only used the Gospel of Matthew. Followed Old Testament customs, and claimed the Apostle Paul was an apostate.
Nicolaitanes	Started by Nicolas (one of the persons full of the Holy Spirit and who had hands laid on by the Apostles in Acts 6:1-6). They practiced ritual adultery, and ate things sacrificed to idols.
Carpocrates	Sorcerer. Practiced ritual fornication. His followers used magical rituals to invoke the aid of demons. Taught reincarnation.

Cerinthus	Claimed Jesus was just a man and that the Christ descended on him at the time of his baptism and left him before he was crucified. Also taught that there would be a literal thousand year reign of Christ on Earth.
Saturninus	Claimed to be an angel, and taught Jesus had no physical body. Also claimed Jesus came to destroy the god of the Old Testament, and claimed that sex, marriage, and reproduction are sinful. Vegetarians. Claimed that marriage and procreation were instituted by Satan.
Marcus	Claimed that the Holy Spirit put a drop of "Her" blood into the wine when he blessed it. Said that his followers would prophecy when they drank the wine. Some believe this is where the doctrine of transubstantiation started. Taught second baptism. Highly mature followers were taught a special incantation that invoked spirits and provided transcendent power.
Marcion	Rejected the Old Testament. Used highly edited versions of Luke and a couple of Paul's epistles. Taught that God is the author of sin, and that there are two equal and opposite gods (i.e.,dualism). Taught that astrology is true, no resurrection from the dead, and his followers should not marry. Claimed Jesus did not have a physical body.

Titian	Adam was not saved; taught soul sleep (that the soul sleeps between death and the resurrection). Also said that it is a sin to use medicine.
Apelles	Said that Jesus came in the flesh; but said that after His resurrection, Jesus disintegrated His own body (which is the same basic teaching as the Jehovahs Witnesses).
Calistus	His followers practiced ritual fornication, common law marriage, and allowed and encouraged drugs to be used to make one sterile and to cause abortions.
Elchasaites	Taught that Jesus reincarnated many times. Cast spells at the baptism of initiates.
Naasseni	Worshiped Satan. Taught that their order was started by James, the brother of Jesus. Claim that Adam was a hermaphrodite. Used the gospel of Thomas (more on this later), and practiced ritual orgies.
Basilides	Taught reincarnation and karma. Sometimes spirits (Including animal spirits) latch onto us and force us to sin. Claimed that Jesus was transformed to look like Simon the Cyrene, and that Simon was crucified in his place. Said that the name of the most supreme god was Abraxas, which is where we get the word Abracadabra (literally, "I bless the dead").

Valentinus	Claimed that those who will be saved were predestined individually before the foundation of the world and that all others were predestined to be damned, but may be able to be saved through doing enough good works. Those predestined to be saved do not need to be concerned with living the Christian life.
Manichaeans	Started by Manes. Founded a religious sect in Persia that incorporated several Gnostic teachings. One of the most famous Manichaeans was Augustine, who eventually left the order and converted to the Catholic church. He brought many Gnostic teachings to the Roman Catholic church, including individual predestination. Later, John Calvin was greatly influenced by the Gnostic teachings of Augustine.

These Gnostics beliefs continue to impact the world (and Christianity) in numerous ways.

Gnostic Scriptures

The Gnostics even began to create their own scriptures, attaching the names of the Apostles of Christ and others to them. Fortunately, the early church was quite familiar with the New Testament Books, and were able to quickly recognize the Gnostics works as forgeries.

One of the largest collections of Gnostic books was discovered in Nag Hammadi, Egypt; yet they are readily seen to be from the early second century (long after the time of Christ).

"The earliest likely date for the Nag Hammadi scrolls is around A.D. 150 and later, when Gnosticism as a system began to flourish. This date is accepted for the Gospels of Philip and Mary." (James L. Garlow and Peter Jones, *Cracking DaVinci's Code: You've Read The Fiction, Now Read The Facts,* 691-695 (Kindle Edition); Colorado Springs, CO; David C. Cook Distribution)

Even one source that is often sympathetic towards the Gnostic scriptures tells us:

"The Nag Hammadi Scriptures is a collection of thirteen papyrus codices—bound books, not scrolls—that were buried near the city of Nag Hammadi in Upper Egypt most likely in the second half of the fourth century CE...

"In all, there are some fifty-two tractates in the collection of Nag Hammadi codices, and since six are duplicates, there are forty-six different texts...

"The precise dates of the composition of these texts are uncertain, but most are from the second and third centuries CE." (James Robinson, in Marvin W. Meyer, *The Nag Hammadi Scriptures,* 159-1677 (Kindle Edition); Harper Collins E-Books)

A Closer Look At Simon Magus And His Probable Connections To The Origin Of Wicca

Let's notice some things which the early church fathers wrote about Simon Magus. (The following quotations are from David Bercot, A Dictionary Of Early Christian Beliefs: A Reference Guide To More Than 700 Topics Discussed By The Early Church Fathers, 22869-22932 (Kindle Edition); Peabody, Massachusetts; Hendrickson Publishers)

"There was a Samaritan, Simon, a native of the village called Gitto, who in the reign of Claudius Caesar, and in your royal city of Rome, did mighty acts of magic.... He was considered a god, and as a god was honored by you with a statue. This statue was erected on the Tiber River, between the two bridges. It bore the following inscription in the language of Rome: "To Simon, the holy God."... And almost all the Samaritans, and a few even of other nations, worship him. They acknowledge him as the first god." (Justin Martyr (c. 160, E), 1.171.)

"The Samaritans, Simon and Menander, did many mighty works by magic and deceived many. They remain deceived. Even among yourselves [i.e., the pagan Romans], as I said before, Simon was in the royal city of Rome in the reign of Claudius Caesar. He so greatly astonished the sacred Senate and the Roman people that he was considered a god. He was honored with a statue, just like the others whom you honor as gods.... I advise you to destroy that statue."(Justin Martyr (c. 160, E), 1.182.)

"When I communicated in writing with Caesar, I gave no thought to any of my people, that is, the Samaritans. Rather, I stated that they were in error to trust in the magician Simon of their own nation. They say that he is God above all power, authority, and might." (Justin Martyr (c. 160, E), 1.260.)

"Simon the Samaritan was the magician of whom Luke, the disciple and follower of the apostles, [writes].... He set himself eagerly to contend against the apostles, in order that he himself might seem to have been a supernatural being. So he applied himself with still greater zeal to the study of the entirety of magic arts, so he could bewilder and overpower multitudes of men. This was his method during the reign of Claudius Caesar, who honored Simon with a statue because of his magical power, according to what is said. This man, then, was glorified by many persons as if he were a god. And he taught that it was himself who appeared among the Jews as the Son.... All sorts of heresies derive their origin from this Simon of Samaria. He formed his sect in the following manner: At Tyre, a city of Phoenicia, he redeemed from slavery a certain woman named Helena. He used to take her along with him. He declared that this woman was the first conception of his mind." (Irenaeus (c. 180, E/ W), 1.347, 348.)

"God will also judge the vain speeches of the perverse Gnostics, by showing that they are the disciples of Simon Magus." (Irenaeus (c. 180, E/ W), 1.507.)

"You install Simon Magus in your Pantheon, giving him a statue and the title of holy God." (Tertullian (c. 197, W), 3.29.)

"The doctrine of Simon's sorcery taught the worship of angels. It was itself actually reckoned among idolatries and condemned by the apostle Peter in Simon's own person." (Tertullian (c. 197, W), 3.259.)

"From that point forward, Simon Magus, who had just become a believer, was cursed by the apostles and ejected from the faith. For he was still thinking somewhat of his juggling sect. That is, he wanted to buy even the gift of the Holy Spirit through imposition of hands, so that he could include it among the miracles of his profession." (Tertullian (c. 200, W), 3.66.)

"There is the Simon of Samaria in the Acts of the Apostles, who bargained for the Holy Spirit. He had only a vain remorse that he and his money must perish together. After his condemnation, he applied his energies to the destruction of the truth, as if to console himself by revenge. In addition to the support with which his own magic arts furnished him, he had recourse to deception. He purchased a Tyrian woman of the name of Helen out of a brothel, with the same money that he had offered for the Holy Spirit—a transaction worthy of the wretched man. He actually pretended that he was the Supreme Father, and he further pretended that the woman was his own Primary Conception." (Tertullian (c. 210, W), 3.215.)

"At this very time, even the heretical dupes of this same Simon are so much elated by the extravagant pretension of their art, that they try to bring up from Hades the souls of the prophets themselves." (Tertullian (c. 210, W), 3.234.)

"The disciples, then, of this [Simon Magus] celebrate magical rites, and they resort to incantations. They transmit both love spells and charms.... This Simon, deceiving many in Samaria by his sorceries, was reproved by the apostles, and he was put under a curse. All of this has been written in the Acts. But Simon afterwards renounced the faith.... And journeying as far as Rome, he came in conflict with the apostles. Peter offered repeated opposition to him, for Simon was deceiving many by his sorceries. (Hippolytus (c. 225, W), 5.80, 81.)

"We know that Simon Magus gave himself the title of the "Power of God." (Origen (c. 228, E), 9.317.)

"[Simon Magus] was successful on that one occasion. But today I think it would be impossible to find thirty of his followers in the entire world. In fact, I am probably overstating the number. There are exceedingly few in Palestine. And in the rest of the world (throughout which he desired to spread the glory of his name), you find him nowhere mentioned. Where his name is found, it is found quoted from the Acts of the Apostles. So he owes the preservation of his name to Christians. This clearly proves that Simon was in no respect divine." (Origen (c. 248, E), 4.422.)

"[Celsus] next pours down upon us a heap of names, saying that he knows of the existence of certain Simonians, who worship Helen... as their teacher. They are called Helenians. However, it has escaped the notice of Celsus that the Simonians do not at all acknowledge Jesus to be the Son of God. Rather, they consider Simon to be the Power of God." (Origen (c. 248, E), 4.570.)

"Simonians are now found [practically] nowhere throughout the world. Yet, in order to gain many followers to himself, Simon protected his disciples from the danger of death [through martyrdom]... by teaching them to regard idolatry as a matter of indifference. So even at the beginning of their existence, the followers of Simon were not exposed to persecution. After all, the wicked demon who was conspiring against the teachings of Jesus was well aware that none of his own teachings would be weakened by the teachings of Simon." (Origen (c. 248, E), 4.578.)

"[The people of Rome] had seen the chariot of Simon Magus, his fiery car, blown into pieces by the mouth of Peter and vanish when Christ was named. They had seen Simon, I say, trusting in false gods. Yet, being abandoned by them in their terror, borne down headlong by his own weight, Simon lay prostrate with his legs broken." (Arnobius (c. 305, E), 6.438.)

"Simon Magus believed and was baptized with many others." (Pamphilus (c. 309, E), 6.167.)

"Simon the magician,... as he flew in the air in an unnatural manner, was dashed against the earth." (Apostolic Constitutions (compiled c. 390, E), 7.401.)

"The first of the new [i.e., Christian] heresies began in this manner: The devil entered into one Simon, a Samaritan of a village called Gitthae. He was a magician by profession.... Simon himself, when he saw the signs and wonders that were done without any magic ceremonies, fell into admiration, believed, was baptized, and continued in fasting and prayer.... But when Simon saw that the Spirit was given to believers by the laying on of hands, he took money and offered it." (Apostolic Constitutions (compiled c. 390, E), 7.452.).

"When he was in Rome, he disturbed the church severely and subverted many, bringing them over to himself. He astonished the Gentiles with his skill in magic." (Apostolic Constitutions (compiled c. 390, E), 7.453; see also 5.143; extended discussion: 5.74–5.81, 7.452–7.453.)

As you can see, the church fathers wrote extensively about Simon Magus!

Here is where it gets very interesting in regards to the connections between Simon and Wicca:

152

"Wicca is a modern derivative of ancient Witchcraft that willingly claims the actual label of "religion." It can be traced directly to the influence of famous occultist Aleister Crowley (1875–1947) and one of his followers, Gerald Gardner (1884–1964), and is centered around the worship of the Lord and Lady, although it includes many other goddesses and gods. It is here, interestingly enough, that the influence of Simon Magus—the sorcerer rebuked by the apostle Peter in Acts 8:9—can be found, indicating a possible ancient source for the roots of Wicca. The Roman historian and bishop Hippolytus (c. 170 AD) described the doctrine of Magus in detail in his Philosophumena: The disciples, then, of this (Magus), celebrate magical rites, and resort to incantations. And (they profess to) transmit both love-spells and charms, and the demons said to be senders of dreams, for the purpose of distracting whomsoever they please.... "And they have an image of Simon (fashioned) into the figure of Jupiter, and (an image) of Helen [Simon's paramour] in the form of Minerva; and they pay adoration to these." But they call the one Lord and the other Lady. And if any one amongst them, on seeing the images of either Simon or Helen, would call them by name, he is cast off, as being ignorant of the mysteries. Wiccans usually practice herbal magic and abide by the Rede doctrine, "An it harm none, do what ye will," and the Threefold Law, which dictates that whatever Wiccans do (whether good or "evil") will return to them at three times the force. This is the Wiccan version of Hindu karma. All Wiccans do not claim to be Witches, and all Witches do not claim to be Wiccan. This is the elusive nature of Neopaganism. Some Wiccans maintain that they do not practice any magick, stating that their focus is only on the Wheel of the Year (observing the eight holidays or sabbats), and personal spirituality. Witches who are not Wiccan abide by the basic creed "Do what you will," minus the "harm none" clause." (Walter Martin, Jill Martin, Rische Kurt Van Gorden, The Kingdom Of The Occult, 9103-9108 (Kindle Edition); Nashville, TN: Thomas Nelson Publishers)

The Bloody History Of The "Goddess"

A study of the "goddess" throughout the Old Testament history is both illuminating and terrifying when considered in light of Wicca.

One former Wiccan, in describing the history of the goddess in ancient society, paints a vivid image:

> ""The Charge" does not tell us what the "due sacrifice" was that the Goddess received in Sparta, but the late Wiccan leader from Great Britain, Alex Sanders, has revealed the nature of the sacrifice. The "youths" were candidates for becoming priests of the Goddess. To prove their worthiness, they were castrated and required to run up to the top of the temple hill carrying their recently severed organs in their hand as an offering to the Goddess. If they made it to the top without fainting or bleeding to death, their wound was cauterized with boiling pitch and they were made priests of the Great Mother. (ouch!) Obviously today, there would be few men wishing to become witches if this practice were being carried on. However, in traditional covens, it is still common for a ceremonial scar to be cut on the perineum of a male initiate. This castration or scarring (called cicatrization) was fairly common in goddess cults of antiquity, as it symbolized a sort of artificial vagina which made the men (who lacked that particular organ) worthy to serve the Goddess. Obviously, this is pretty grisly stuff, especially in light of some of the historical practices we have mentioned. Can we really believe that a Goddess who demanded "due sacrifice" in the past is not doing so today? With all the whipping and "suffering in order to learn" going on in the covens, I would say that the statement that the Goddess demands no sacrifice rings a bit hollow. All we are doing here is presenting the fact that the sweet "Gentle Goddess" image that most witches are fed by their teachers is not borne out by history. This Goddess has a bloody, savage and vindictive side which cannot be ignored, especially in the light of what the Bible has to say about her....

"The Goddess first appears in the Bible by name in the days of King Solomon. Although he was noted for his piety and his wisdom, Solomon seems to have started to hang around with the wrong kind of women in his later years (around 984 B.C.). He married pagan women (1 Kings 11:1), which was forbidden by God, and they dragged their pagan gods and goddesses into the family with them....

"Although most witches know this, I should point out that Ashtoreth is an older form of the name Asherah or Astarte, one of the names found in the beginning invocation of the Drawing Down the Moon ceremony. So again, we are discussing an important and significant "version" or archetype of the "gentle" goddess of Wicca. We need to understand three things about these verses. First, almost all of what is contained in them describes modern goddess-worship: the rituals on high hills and under "every green tree;" the talk of worshiping the host of heaven; and of course, divination and enchantments, which are all part and parcel of modern Wicca. Divination is anything like astrology or tarot cards; and enchantment is magic spells. Secondly, although some Pagan groups call themselves "groves," the term refers to an "Asherah pole" or an idol to Ashtoreth or Asherah, the goddess! Thus, we are hearing a report of the worship of one of the oldest forms of the goddess and her consort (in this case, Molech or Ba'al). Thirdly, this "passing their sons and daughters through the fire" referred to a gruesome method of infant sacrifice done to the goddess and god. The idol representing the god had flames within it, which were stoked up and heated the idol's form to a scorching surface temperature. The child being sacrificed was placed in the blistering arms of the idol and burned alive! Is it any wonder that God forbade the Israelites from worshiping the goddess?...Although "white" witches and other goddess worshipers today will loudly deny that they practice infant sacrifice; all they have done is institutionalize and legalize the practice. You will find that Wiccans are at the forefront of the movement to preserve the right of a woman to kill her baby through abortion. We

155

ask ourselves, "What kind of parent would take their baby and fry it alive in the lap of an idol?" Yet our culture has accepted quite complacently the burning (with saline solution) or dismemberment (with suction) of babies in abortion clinics by the tens of millions! As a witch, I was militantly "Pro-choice....

"I now find it difficult to understand the moral differences between the goddess worshipers of the past who offered their babies on the altars of Ashtoreth or Ba'al and the Wiccan goddess worshipers today who work vigorously for the maintenance of their right to offer their babies on the altars of the abortionist....

"We should not be surprised to see Wiccans at the vanguard of the pro-abortion picket lines. After all, the first abortionists in history were probably witches. As a witch myself, I knew of half a dozen herbal "potions" which could induce spontaneous abortions." (William Schnoebelen, Wicca: Satan's Little White Lie, 1103-1158 (Kindle Edition); Ontario, CA; Chick Publications)

When we consider the history of blood and human sacrifice tied in with the "older" forms of Wicca, it should certainly cause us to take pause and consider the "newer" form to determine if there really is as much difference between the two as we are often told that there is by Wiccan today.

"Elementals"

Another important part of Wiccan belief deals with "elementals."

Wiccans generally believe that everything in nature is able to be broken down into the basic "elemental" forces of earth, air, water, fire (and the fifth element of "spirit," or *Akashi,* from which the other four elements were formed).

It is further believed by some Wiccans that ancestral spirits can merge with these elementals after successive stages of death and reincarnation, and that these basic "elemental" powers may be harnessed through the use of magic (which involves incantations, use of hallucinogenic drugs, coven meetings, and ritualistic sex).

This, of course, raises the interesting parallel of the "elementals" that the New Testament speaks of. Several passages of the New Testament hint of these "elemental spirits" in various forms (see Colossians 2:8, 20; Galatians 4:3, 9).

> *Galatians 4:3 (LEB)-So also we, when we were children, we were enslaved under the elemental spirits of the world.*

> *Galatians 4:3 (TPT)-So it is with us. When we were juveniles we were enslaved under the hostile spirits of the world.*

Of particular interest is the Greek word *stoicheia,* translated as "elemental spirits," and "hostile spirits,." In some translations of the Bible, we read this word being translated as "basic principles of the world" (NKJV, NASB).

Scholar Clinton Arnold, in discussing the linguistic and etymological nuances of the word, has written:

> "The interpretation of stoicheia as personal spiritual entities is the most compelling view. Consequently this interpretation has commanded the consent of the majority of commentators in the history of the interpretation of the passages.12 This view is based partly on the widespread usage of stoicheia for astral spirits in the second and third centuries A.D. (and probably before)....

> "It is important to realize that not only pagans used this word to refer to spirits, but Jews also used this word in that sense. The Jewish Testament of Solomon, written during the Roman Imperial period, includes five references to stoicheia as spirit beings....

> "These terms further reflect the wide array of vocabulary in reference to spirit beings, shared by Jews and Gentiles alike. Paul drew from this reservoir of terminology with which his readers would be readily familiar. He showed no interest, however, in discussing what he believed to be true about the starry host. Rather, he lumped all manner of spirits together, affirmed Christ's superiority, and encouraged

believers to be prepared for their hostile intentions and attacks by reminding minding his readers of their past ability to enslave." (Clinton E. Arnold, *Powers Of Darkness: Principalities & Powers In Paul's Letters,* 53-54 (Kindle Edition); Downers Grove, Illinois; InterVarsity Press)

Quite often in the pre-Flood religions, these spiritual powers were accessed through objects known as teraphim. There were two basic types of teraphim.

The first type of teraphim utilized the skull of the firstborn male of a family. Believing that the spirit would stay connected to the skull, the ancients would attempt to harness the power of the spirit for knowledge and personal gain or retribution.

The second type of teraphim was the creation of a doll which resembled a deceased human. These idols needed to be used at precise times (and hence, astrology played a major part in the ceremonies). It was also important to have candles, ritualistic knives and occult based objects in the ceremony to harness these elemental powers.

We read of some of these things in the ancient book of Jasher (a book which is not inspired, but which is "recommended reading" by the Bible-see Joshua 10:13):

> Jasher 31:41-43—"And this is the manner of the images; in taking a man who is the first born and slaying him and taking the hair off his head, and taking salt and salting the head and anointing it in oil, then taking a small tablet of copper or a tablet of gold and writing the name upon it, and placing the tablet under his tongue, and taking the head with the tablet under the tongue and putting it in the house, and lighting up lights before it and bowing down to it. And at the time when they bow down to it, it speaketh to them in all matters that they ask of it, through the power of the name which is written in it. And some make them in the figures of men, of gold and silver, and go to them in times known to them, and the figures receive the influence of the stars, and

tell them future things, and in this manner were the images which Rachel stole from her father, Laban."

The spiritual forces that are harnessed in Wicca are very real, and the Word of God identifies these powers as wicked spirits that are opposed to God and His Word.

Conclusion

Wicca is an ancient religion that is based on various forms of paganism, which were introduced to mankind before the Global Flood, and which have continued throughout every time and culture in various religions and traditions.

The grace of the Lord Jesus Christ, and the love of God, and the communion of the Holy Spirit be with you all. amen.

Questions

1. Describe the basic teachings of the Gnostics.
   _____
   _____
   _____

2. What are teraphim and what were they used for?
   _____
   _____
   _____

3. Describe the dating of the Gnostic books.
   _____
   _____
   _____

4. Who do some believe started the religion known as Wicca?
   _____

5. Read Acts 8:4-13. Many people had for a long time believed in Simon, but when they saw Philip and the kingdom of God, they saw such a difference that they believed in Jesus Christ and were baptized. What are

some lessons this teaches us about the differences
between paganism and Christianity?

_____

_____

_____

_____

6. What are some reasons for understanding stoichea to be
spirits?

_____

_____

_____

_____

7. Using the writings of the church fathers, provide a
description of Simon the Sorcerer.

_____

_____

_____

_____

_____

_____

Lesson Seven

Conclusion

We have briefly examined some of the major pagan religions that are growing in the United States and abroad.

Now, we must turn our attention to perhaps the most aspect of all religion: the Afterlife.

Reincarnation

In every one of the religions that we have investigated, the primary teaching of the afterlife involves reincarnation. This is the belief that after a person dies, his soul is brought back to physical life again, where he will then live and die and continue the process of reincarnation.

For example, Wiccans teach that at death a person's soul goes to a realm known as "Summerland." After this, they are reincarnated back into the world of man.

Cunningham describes:

> "What happens after death? Only the body dies. The soul lives on. Some Wiccans say that it journeys to a realm variously known as the Land of the Faerie, the Shining Land, and the Land of the Young. This realm is neither in heaven nor the underworld. It simply is—a nonphysical reality much less dense than ours. Some Wiccan traditions describe it as a land of eternal summer, with grassy fields and sweet flowing rivers, perhaps the earth before the advent of humans. Others see it vaguely as a realm without forms, where energy swirls coexist with the greatest energies—the Goddess and God in their celestial identities. The soul is said to review the past life, perhaps through some mysterious way with the deities. This isn't a judgment, a weighing of one's soul, but an incarnational review.

Lessons learned or ignored are brought to light. After the proper time, when the conditions on earth are correct, the soul is reincarnated and life begins again. The final question—what happens after the last incarnation? Wiccan teachings have always been vague on this. Basically, the Wiccans say that after rising upon the spiral of life and death and rebirth, those souls who have attained perfection break away from the cycle forever and dwell with the Goddess and God. Nothing is ever lost. The energies resident in our souls return to the divine source from which they originally emanated. Because of their acceptance of reincarnation, the Wicca don't fear death as a final plunge into oblivion, the days of life on earth forever behind them. It is seen as the door to birth. Thus our very lives are symbolically linked with the endless cycles of the seasons that shape our planet." (Scott Cunningham, Wicca: A Guide for the Solitary Practitioner, 98-99 (Kindle Edition); St. Paul, Minnesota; Llewelyn Publications)

Many in our day and age subscribe to the theory of reincarnation. Usually, evidences for reincarnation come from what is known as "past-life recall." This is the situation where a person (whether involuntarily or in response to hypnotic trance) recalls events of an event which he believes is a past life.

Ian Stevenson was one of the foremost researchers on the topic of past life studies. While being an avid defender of the theory of reincarnation, he acknowledged there are many potential explanations for "past-life recall" besides a person actually living a past life. In his works, he discussed such potential explanations as ESP (extra sensory perception) and genetic memory.

However, two of the explanations that he offers for alleged past-life experiences should be considered in greater detail.

Cryptomnesia

This is where a person learns something, and then forgets it; only to have the memory triggered later but with no memory of where the memory originally came from.

"In some of the cases, e.g., Wijerante, Marta, William George, Jr., Norman Despers, and Corliss Chotkin, Jr., members of the child's family already know most or all of the facts stated by the child. Cryptomnesia may suffice in these cases as an explanation for all, or nearly all, of the informational aspects of the cases, although it will not, I think, suffice to explain other features of some of these cases, e.g., the behavioral features or the birthmarks.... I do not think we can ever exclude absolutely some earlier normal communications of information to these children. I agree with Chari that unless we can do so there always remains some possibility that cryptomnesia accounts for the cases..." (Ian Stevenson, Twenty Cases Suggestive of Reincarnation, 334, 339; Charlottesville and London: University Of Virginia Press)

Even later in in life, Stevenson acknowledged that he was often surprised by how often cryptomnesia may account for alleged past-life recall:

"A person who obtains some information normally and later forgets that he has done so is said to show "cryptomnesia" or "source amnesia." (I described and gave examples of this in chapter 3.) I consider the possibility of cryptomnesia in almost every case I study. The results of inquiries have occasionally surprised me. As I have penetrated a case more deeply, I have sometimes found that, even though the two immediate families were unacquainted before the case developed, they turned out to have one or more mutual friends; in other instances, they had more possibilities for indirect communication with each other than they had earlier realized. In the last chapter I mentioned three cases (those of Sunita Khandelwal, Pushpa, and Parmod Sharma) in which the two families concerned had had (or might have had) some slight contact with each other. I found no evidence in any of these cases that information about the previous personality had passed from one family to the other, but I could not decisively exclude the possibility that this had happened." (Ian Stevenson, M.D.,

Children Who Remember Previous Lives: A Question of Reincarnation, rev. ed., 153 (Kindle Edition); Jefferson, North Carolina; McFarland & Company, Inc., Publishers)

Another investigator has provided remarkable detail on this as well:

"Bridey Murphy's knowledge of Irish history and customs was almost certainly an instance stance of "cryptomnesia" or source amnesia in which the subjects obtain their knowledge through normal channels but are unable to recall them. Harold Rosen, a Canadian psychiatrist, describes the case of a patient who, under hypnosis, started writing in Oscan, a language spoken in Western Italy up to the first century B.C.E. The patient denied having ever seen the words he had written and also insisted that he had never so much as heard of Oscan. When rehypnotized, however, he recalled sitting in the library while somebody next to him opened a book on a page that contained the Oscan "Curse of Vibia." It was this Oscan curse that he had reproduced. Numerous similar cases are on record. One of them concerns a woman referred to as Miss C., going back to 1906. It was investigated for the British Society for Psychical Research by the well-known classical scholar G. Lowes Dickinson who, after considerable effort, traced his subject's remarkably detailed knowledge of the personalities at the court of Richard II to her reading of a historical novel as a child. As a result of the work of Dickinson and the more recent research of Edwin S. Zolik of Marquette University," the Finnish psychiatrist Reima Kampman, Melvin Harris, and the psychologists N. P. Spanos, Robert Baker, and J. Venn, this phenomenon has been completely demystified." (Paul Edwards, Reincarnation: A Critical Examination, 1003-1009 (Kindle Edition); Amherst, New York; Prometheus Books)

Influence From Disembodied Spirits

Perhaps the most disturbing possibility that may account for some past-life recall is the influence of demonic spirits. Describing Stevenson's research, Wall and Barlow write:

> "He provided an alternative, one he claimed should be taken seriously: "Possession of the living by a foreign spirit." This can't be overstated: One of the world's top research scientists in the field acknowledged that a foreign spirit could occupy a living person. Gary Habermas, a Christian scholar, is quick to caution that Stevenson is not suggesting demonic possession. Instead, Stevenson is explaining the phenomenon as possession by the disembodied "spirit of the actual person who had previously died." Stevenson himself acknowledges that "the distinction between reincarnation and possession becomes blurred." Here is how he defines the terms:... if the previous personality seems to associate itself with the physical organism at the time of conception or during embryonic development we speak of reincarnation; if the association between previous personality and physical organism only comes later, we speak of possession. It's possible that what we think of as reincarnation is really a foreign spirit taking hold of, or possessing, a living person. This causes the person to think he or she was someone else in a previous life. Habermas observes: Researchers and theorists have not proved that these cases demand reincarnation.... There are several cases where either discarnate or demonic possession serves as the best explanation and seems to be accepted as such by most researchers, including Stevenson himself. Sometimes the deceased person (supposedly reincarnated) died after the birth of the individual who was later influenced. This sequence dispels any notion of "I died" and then "I was reborn." The timing is simply off. As Stevenson says, "No matter how you look at it, reincarnation gets the short end of the evidential stick." Xenoglossy, or speaking a previously unlearned language, can be accounted for by possession, so it doesn't constitute solid evidence for

reincarnation. Neither does sharing birthmarks or a physical defect with a dead person. Stevenson cites mystics who sometimes develop stigmata, or wounds corresponding to those suffered by Jesus on the cross. Having those wounds does not make them reincarnations of Jesus. Similarity does not prove sameness." (Keith Wall & James L. Barlow, Heaven and the Afterlife, 235-236 (Kindle Edition); Bloomington, Minnesota; Bethany House Publishers)

Even noted reincarnation supporters acknowledge the fact that documented cases have been made of people who were believed to have been reincarnated, but were instead under influence of possessing spirits.

For example:

"Having said that, there are a few rare but well-documented cases that suggest spirit possession can occur, in which case it could be argued that the same phenomenon could be happening with children who appear to remember a past life. There are, however, important differences. One of the earliest cases, which occurred in the USA in 1877, involved Mary Lurancy Vennum, who at the age of thirteen appeared to be possessed by two different entities. The first was described as a sullen old hag, whereas the next was a young man who had run away from home. At this point, it sounds very much like a case of multiple personality disorder. Her parents were introduced to a hypnotist who induced a trance and spoke to Mary's "sane and happy" mind, which told him that "an angel" named Mary Roff wanted to replace the other two. Sure enough, Roff not only appeared but took over Mary's body completely. The possessing spirit was easily identified: She was the daughter of the people who had recommended the hypnotist and had died when she was just one year old. This possession was so total that Mary Lurancy Vennum went to live with the Roffs, until, three months and ten days after she appeared, Mary Roff suddenly disappeared and the teenager returned to her natural parents. This case is not unique. Two similar cases, but with different outcomes, have been investigated

166

in the twentieth century—both in India. The first involved a young married woman, Sumitra Singh, who in 1982, soon after the birth of a son, had suffered fits and then began speaking as if she were three other people, two of them women (one a goddess, the other a woman who had drowned) and the third an unidentified man. It was the goddess, Santoshi Ma, who announced in 1985 that Sumitra would die in three days' time. That is precisely what appeared to happen and her family testified that her body had no pulse for three-quarters of an hour. Then, as preparations began for her funeral, she suddenly revived... not as Sumitra, but as Shiva, who claimed to have been the mother of two children and who was murdered by her in-laws. Shiva remained for the rest of her life in Sumitra's body, writing letters to her natural father complaining that "God has dumped me here" in Sumitra's body and in a dirty home, which she compared unfavorably to her previous existence. Shiva's spirit has since died a second time, following the death of Sumitra, whose body she had taken over. This fascinating case was recently re-investigated by Antonia Mills and is the subject of a lengthy report in the Society for Psychical Research's Proceedings.

"A very similar and remarkable transformation, but without a death apparently occurring, was experienced in 1974 by a thirty-two-year-old unmarried woman, Uttara Huddar, who awoke one day in her home in Nagpur, in west-central India, and instead of speaking Marathi, her native tongue, began speaking a language her parents could not understand. Her personality had also changed and she called herself Sharada. Others recognized the language she spoke as Bengali, which Uttara had never learned. This was extremely disturbing for the family, naturally, and also for Sharada, who could not understand why she was suddenly in a different place. However, it was not a permanent change. The Sharada personality "appears" for different periods, from one day to six weeks, and then Uttara repossesses her body again. Each personality, when it takes control of the body, is oblivious to the existence of the other.

This may sound like a form of multiple personality disorder, but it seems Sharada did once enjoy a totally separate existence, living between 1810 and 1830 and dying from a snake bite on her toe. Also, she provided investigators with details of her Bengal family and they were able to trace its genealogical records and confirm information she gave. Lastly, her ability to speak Bengali—a phenomenon known as xenoglossy—would also appear to rule out the possibility that the "intruder" is just an aspect of Uttara's personality. Sharada, incidentally, said she had no idea where she had been since her death. If the Sumitra/Shiva and Uttara/Sharada cases are as reported—and both have been investigated by seasoned reincarnation researchers—they would seem to offer unusual, even unique, variations on a reincarnation theme in which, for whatever reason, a soul either replaces another in an adult body, or takes on a shared "tenancy" with the original owner." (Roy Stemman, The Big Book of Reincarnation: Examining the Evidence that We Have All Lived Before, 203-205 (Kindle Edition); San Antonio, TX; Hierophant Publishing)

Recently, Lee Strobel interviewed Douglas Groothuis on the subject of reincarnation. Notice this snippet from their conversation regarding xenoglossy and reincarnation:

"Of course. And sometimes we may need to consider other possibilities." "Such as?" "Demonic influence or possession of some sort," he said. "Certainly the Bible affirms that this sort of thing can happen. And since reincarnation pulls people away from the Christian gospel, there would be a motivation for dark forces to fan those flames." Philosopher Gary Habermas reports the case of a novelist who said she had been reincarnated more than a dozen times. Only later was it revealed that she had been provided historical details through her personal link to a spirit. Said Habermas, "This suggests... that the so-called evidences for reincarnation could be coming from deceptive nonhuman spirit beings."" (Douglas Groothius, in Lee Strobel, The Case for Heaven: A Journalist Investigates

Evidence for Life After Death, 201-202 (Kindle Edition); Grand Rapids, Michigan; Zondervan)

Reincarnation does not provide an adequate explanation to the question, "What happens when we die?"

Looking At The Bible

Through our studies, we have noticed a few examples of evidence which show that the Bible is the Word of God (i.e., evidences from prophecy and fulfillment, miraculous attestation, and archaeological corroboration of numerous supernatural events recorded in the Bible). There is an unshakable amount of evidence which demonstrates that the Bible is the Word of God, as it claims:

> *2 Timothy 3:16-17—All Scripture is given by inspiration of God, and is profitable for doctrine, for reproof, for correction, for instruction in righteousness, (17) that the man of God may be complete, thoroughly equipped for every good work.*

Christians do not accept the Bible as the Word of God because of blind faith; instead our faith is grounded in words that are true and reasonable (Acts 26:25). Jesus provided "many infallible proofs" that He had risen from the dead (Acts 1:3), and God calls upon us to use logic and rational thinking as we "reason" with Him (Isaiah 1:18) and while we "test all things; hold fast to that which is good" (1 Thessalonians 5:21).

With that in mind, what does the Bible teach us about death?

Mankind has a spirit within him, an immaterial element that survives the death of the body.

> *Ecclesiastes 12:7—Then the dust will return to the earth as it was, And the spirit will return to God who gave it.*

> *Matthew 10:28—And do not fear those who kill the body but cannot kill the soul. But rather fear Him who is able to destroy both soul and body in hell.*

Modern science demonstrates the truthfulness of the Bible in regard to the existence of the human soul. One author has written:

"Increasingly, however, toward the end of the last century, even leading physical scientists such as physicists, chemists, physiologists—and especially neurologists— began to see that materialism did not explain the data that was coming in. Inescapably, it all pointed to a nonphysical source of thought. Mind had to be distinct from brain. Chemical and electrical reactions in the brain could not explain the whole person. Eccles pointedly observed, "It is not at all clear how 'natural selection 'has somehow selected for Bach's 'Partitas.'.. or for a system of justice that will let a thousand guilty men go free lest one innocent man be constrained of his liberties." After extensive interviews in Europe and America, philosophy-of-science professor John Gliedman wrote: Several leading theorists have arrived at the same startling conclusions: their work suggests a hidden spiritual world, within all of us....

"From Berkeley to Paris and from London to Princeton, prominent scientists from fields as diverse as neurophysiology and quantum physics are coming out of the closet and admitting they believe in the possibility, at least, of such unscientific entities as the immortal human spirit and divine creation. Materialistic science has nothing to say about the mind (except to deny its existence), which famed neurosurgeon Wilder Penfield described as "outside [and] independent of the brain." Penfield, during his lifetime known as "the greatest living Canadian," taught for years at Montreal's McGill University and the Royal Victoria hospital. Obviously, anything governing human behavior that is outside and independent of the brain must be nonphysical—a scientific conclusion confirmed by many experiments that rankles materialists. Sir John Eccles confirms, with his own research, Penfield's conclusions. He describes the brain as a machine that a ghost can operate, by which he ordinarily means the human spirit." (Dave Hunt, Cosmos, Creator, And Human Destiny: Answering Darwin, Dawkins, And The New Atheists, 4358-4371 (Kindle Edition); Bend, Oregon; The Berean Call)

Eben Alexander III is a world-renowned neurosurgeon who had a truly remarkable experience that is worthy of consideration.

As he recounts:

> "As much as I'd grown up wanting to believe in God and Heaven and an afterlife, my decades in the rigorous scientific world of academic neurosurgery had profoundly called into question how such things could exist....In fact, I would have loved to have enjoyed some of it myself. The older I got, however, the less likely that seemed. Like an ocean wearing away a beach, over the years my scientific worldview gently but steadily undermined my ability to believe in something larger. Science seemed to be providing a steady onslaught of evidence that pushed our significance in the universe ever closer to zero. Belief would have been nice. But science is not concerned with what would be nice. It's concerned with what is." (Eben Alexander III M.D., Proof of Heaven: A Neurosurgeon's Journey into the Afterlife, 34-35 (Kindle Edition); New York, NY; Simon & Schuster)

Something happened, however, which convinced the good doctor that there is good evidence for the afterlife.

> "On November 10, 2008, however, at age fifty-four, my luck seemed to run out. I was struck by a rare illness and thrown into a coma for seven days. During that time, my entire neocortex—the outer surface of the brain, the part that makes us human—was shut down. Inoperative. In essence, absent. When your brain is absent, you are absent, too. As a neurosurgeon, I'd heard many stories over the years of people who had strange experiences, usually after suffering cardiac arrest: stories of traveling to mysterious, wonderful landscapes; of talking to dead relatives—even of meeting God Himself. Wonderful stuff, no question. But all of it, in my opinion, was pure fantasy. What caused the otherworldly types of experiences that such people so often report? I didn't claim to know, but I did know that they were brain-based. All of consciousness is. If you don't have a

working brain, you can't be conscious. This is because the brain is the machine that produces consciousness in the first place. When the machine breaks down, consciousness stops. As vastly complicated and mysterious as the actual mechanics of brain processes are, in essence the matter is as simple as that. Pull the plug and the TV goes dead. The show is over, no matter how much you might have been enjoying it. Or so I would have told you before my own brain crashed. During my coma my brain wasn't working improperly—it wasn't working at all. I now believe that this might have been what was responsible for the depth and intensity of the near-death experience (NDE) that I myself underwent during it. Many of the NDEs reported happen when a person's heart has shut down for a while. In those cases, the neocortex is temporarily inactivated, but generally not too damaged, provided that the flow of oxygenated blood is restored through cardiopulmonary resuscitation or reactivation of cardiac function within four minutes or so. But in my case, the neocortex was out of the picture. I was encountering the reality of a world of consciousness that existed completely free of the limitations of my physical brain. Mine was in some ways a perfect storm of near-death experiences. As a practicing neurosurgeon with decades of research and hands-on work in the operating room behind me, I was in a better-than-average position to judge not only the reality but also the implications of what happened to me. Those implications are tremendous beyond description. My experience showed me that the death of the body and the brain are not the end of consciousness, that human experience continues beyond the grave. More important, it continues under the gaze of a God who loves and cares about each one of us and about where the universe itself and all the beings within it are ultimately going." (Eben Alexander III M.D., Proof of Heaven: A Neurosurgeon's Journey into the Afterlife, 8-9 (Kindle Edition); New York, NY; Simon & Schuster)

Strobel discusses Alexander in his aforementioned book, The Case For Heaven.

Consider this:

"As a Harvard neurosurgeon and an agnostic, Eben Alexander believed we are just our brains, nothing more. "If you don't have a working brain, you can't be conscious," he said. "This is because the brain is the machine that produces consciousness in the first place. When the machine breaks down, consciousness stops... Pull the plug and the TV goes dead. The show is over, no matter how much you might have been enjoying it." In short, no afterlife, no heaven, no existence of any kind beyond the grave. Then came November 10, 2008, when a rare brain infection crashed his entire neocortex, the part of the brain that makes us human. "During my coma my brain wasn't working improperly—it wasn't working at all," he would say later. While his brain wasn't functioning, he still found himself fully conscious, but now in a "brilliant, vibrant, ecstatic, stunning" new world—a place fueled by an exhilarating sense of unconditional love. There he encountered the face of a beautiful girl who gazed at him with an enigmatic smile. He had no idea who she was, but she radiated a beautiful love toward him. Miraculously, the physician emerged fully healed from his near-death experience. He had been adopted as a baby, and after reconnecting with his birth family, he was sent a photograph—it was a picture of a sister named Betsy whom he had never known anything about and who had died years earlier. The photo floored him. This was the girl with the mysterious smile who had exuded such love to him in the world beyond. "My experience showed me that the death of the body and the brain are not the end of consciousness, that human experience continues beyond the grave," he now declares. "More important, it continues under the gaze of a God who loves and cares about each one of us."". (The Case for Heaven: A Journalist Investigates Evidence for Life After Death, 49-50 (Kindle Edition); Grand Rapids, Michigan; Zondervan)

There IS a reality which exists beyond the material realm (just as the Bible teaches).

173

What Everything Boils Down To

Christians do not rely on near-death experiences to confirm the truthfulness of the Christian religion. Our Source of this knowledge comes directly from the Son of God, Whose resurrection from the dead documents His words (Romans 1:4).

According to the Bible, mankind is in a serious spiritual situation because of sin. When a person chooses to violate the will of Heaven, He separates himself from God:

> *Isaiah 59:1-2—Behold, the LORD's hand is not shortened, That it cannot save; Nor His ear heavy, That it cannot hear. (2) But your iniquities have separated you from your God; And your sins have hidden His face from you, So that He will not hear.*

Since God is perfectly holy in His Nature, He cannot abide our sin:

> *Habakkuk 1:13—You are of purer eyes than to behold evil, And cannot look on wickedness....*

Because people sin, they are condemned to separation from Hell:

> *Matthew 25:41—Then He will also say to those on the left hand, 'Depart from Me, you cursed, into the everlasting fire prepared for the devil and his angels:*

> *2 Thessalonians 1:9—These shall be punished with everlasting destruction from the presence of the Lord and from the glory of His power,*

According to Scripture, when Jesus returns, the Day of Judgment will take place.

> *Acts 17:30-31—Truly, these times of ignorance God overlooked, but now commands all men everywhere to repent, (31) because He has appointed a day on which He will judge the world in righteousness by the Man whom He has ordained. He has given assurance of this to all by raising Him from the dead."*

If this were the end of the story, we would not have any hope of a "happy ending!"

The Good News Of Jesus Christ

God, in His holiness, could not overlook our sin; but in HIs love, He made a way for us to be saved. God's Son was incarnated into the world.

> *1 Timothy 3:16—And without controversy great is the mystery of godliness: God was manifested in the flesh, Justified in the Spirit, Seen by angels, Preached among the Gentiles, Believed on in the world, Received up in glory.*

Jesus Christ came on a mission-a mission to pay the guilt of our sins by offering Himself in our place. Since He never sinned (Hebrews 4:15), He was able to become the perfect Sacrifice for sinful man.

> *John 3:16-17—For God so loved the world that he gave his only begotten son, that whoever believes in him should not perish but have everlasting life. (17) for God did not send his son into the world to condemn the world, but that the world through him might be saved.*

After Jesus' death, He was buried; and three days later, He arose from the dead!

> *1 Corinthians 15:1-8—Moreover, brethren, I declare to you the gospel which I preached to you, which also you received and in which you stand, (2) by which also you are saved, if you hold fast that word which I preached to you—unless you believed in vain. (3) For I delivered to you first of all that which I also received: that Christ died for our sins according to the Scriptures, (4) and that He was buried, and that He rose again the third day according to the Scriptures, (5) and that He was seen by Cephas, then by the twelve. (6) After that He was seen by over five hundred brethren at once, of whom the greater part remain to the present, but some have fallen asleep. (7) After that He was seen by James, then by all the*

apostles. (8) Then last of all He was seen by me also, as by one born out of due time.

God has a simple plan by which we are saved from our sins.

Those who believe in Jesus Christ are told:

Acts 2:38—Then Peter said to them, "Repent, and let every one of you be baptized in the name of Jesus Christ for the remission of sins; and you shall receive the gift of the Holy Spirit.

To repent means to turn your focus from the world and turn to God. It doesn't mean to get everything wrong in your life worked out (as many suppose). It means that you are making Jesus Chris the Lord of your heart and life, and He will help you to make the changes to your life that you need.

Luke 9:23-26—Then He said to them all, "If anyone desires to come after Me, let him deny himself, and take up his cross daily, and follow Me. (24) For whoever desires to save his life will lose it, but whoever loses his life for My sake will save it. (25) For what profit is it to a man if he gains the whole world, and is himself destroyed or lost? (26) For whoever is ashamed of Me and My words, of him the Son of Man will be ashamed when He comes in His own glory, and in His Father's, and of the holy angels.

To be baptized means to be immersed (submerged) in water.

It is in baptism that the repentant believer:

- Is Saved (Mark 16:15-16);
- Is Fully Initiated As A Disciple Of Christ (Matthew 28:19);
- Is Purchased By The Godhead (Matthew 28:19);
- Comes Into Full Fellowship With The Trinity (Matthew 28:19);
- Is Born Again (John 3:5);
- Is Added To The Kingdom/Church (John 3:5; Acts 2:47);
- Receives The Remission Of Sins (Acts 2:38);

- Receives The Gift Of The Holy Spirit (Acts 2:38);
- Obeys The Command Of The Lord (Acts 10:47-48);
- Has Sins Washed Away (Acts 22:16);
- Is Buried With Christ (Romans 6:3-4);
- Is Raised To Walk In Newness Of Life (Romans 6:3-4);
- Becomes A Slave Of Righteousness (Romans 6:17-18);
- Is Baptized Into The Leadership Of Christ (1 Corinthians 10:1-5);
- Is Added To The Body Of Christ (1 Corinthians 12:13);
- Is Made To Drink Of The One Spirit (1 Corinthians 12:13);
- Receives The Assurance Of Being With Other Baptized Believers In Eternity (1 Corinthians 15:29);
- Enters Into Christ (Galatians 3:26-27);
- Becomes A Child Of God (Galatians 3:26-37);
- Is Saved By Faith (Galatians 3:26-27);
- Puts On Christ (Galatians 3:26-27);
- Enters Into The Unity Of Baptized Believers (Ephesians 4:4-6);
- Receives The Circumcision Of Christ Through Faith In The Working Of God (Colossians 2:12-14);
- Buried With Christ To Be Able To Seek Those Things Which Are Above (Colossians 2:12-3:4);
- Receives The Washing Of Regeneration (Titus 3:4-7);
- Receives The Renewing Of The Holy Spirit (Titus 3:4-7);
- Receive The Washing Of The Body (Hebrews 10:22);
- Is Given The Clean Conscience (Hebrews 10:22);
- Is Saved Like Noahs (I Peter 3:18-22);

- Pleads For A Clean Conscience To God (1 Peter 3:21);

- Makes A Pledge Of A Good Conscience Toward God (1 Peter 3:21);

- Joins In The Witness Of Christ's Baptism Before God (1 John 5:5-8)

When a baptized believer (i.e., a Christian) sins against God, he is able to go directly to God in prayer as he repents:

> *Hebrews 4:15-16—For we do not have a High Priest who cannot sympathize with our weaknesses, but was in all points tempted as we are, yet without sin. (16) Let us therefore come boldly to the throne of grace, that we may obtain mercy and find grace to help in time of need.*

> *1 John 1:9— If we confess our sins, He is faithful and just to forgive us our sins and to cleanse us from all unrighteousness.*

If you need to be baptized into Christ, please do not delay.

The churches of Christ stand ready to assist you!

The grace of the Lord Jesus Christ, and the love of God, and the communion of the Holy Spirit, be with you all. Amen.

Questions

1. What is cryptomnesia, and how does it relate to the study of reincarnation?

2. What are some of the evidences that Jesus Christ arose from the dead on the third day after His death? Consider 1 Corinthians 15:1-8 in your response.

3. Consider Acts 17:30-31. What will happen when Jesus returns?

_____
_____

4. How may demonic influence relate to the subject of reincarnation? Be specific in your response.

_____
_____
_____
_____

5. According to Acts 2:38, what two things must a believer in Jesus do in order to be forgiven of sins?

_____
_____
_____

6. If we want to be saved, we must take up our
_____ and follow _____
(Luke 9:23).

7. What are some of the benefits associated in the New Testament with baptism?

_____
_____
_____
_____
_____
_____

Other Books by Mark Tabata You Will Enjoy

- *Reincarnation: Fact or Fiction?*

- *Old Apologetics for a New Age: Does God Exist?*

- *Old Apologetics for a New Age: Inspiration of the Bible*

All available at Amazon.com and CobbPublishing.com